An
Introduction
to
SHARED
INQUIRY

SCHOOL OF EDUCATION
CURRICULUM LABORATORY
UM-DEARBORN

An
Introduction
to
SHARED
INQUIRY

SCHOOL OF EDUCATION
CURRICULUM LABORATORY
UM-DEARBORN

The Great Books Foundation
A nonprofit educational corporation

- anyone can host a program at least 24 people

Video - parents education
3 groups call
discussing stories used

Instructor Shawn Yardley
1-800-222-5870
9-5 Chicago

- rent or purchase

Designed by Darcie Sanders/Airborne Associates
Northbrook, Illinois

Copyright © 1987 by The Great Books Foundation
Chicago, Illinois
ISBN 0-945159-50-1

Second Printing

9 8 7 6 5 4 3 2 1 0

Published and distributed by

The Great Books Foundation
A nonprofit educational corporation
40 East Huron Street
Chicago, Illinois 60611

Contents

Shared Inquiry

READING serious literature is a collaboration—a meeting of minds—between author and reader. The author provides the completed work, but doesn't tell the reader what to think about it: the reader must strive to understand, to interpret, what the author is saying. It is this interpretive process that is the focus of shared inquiry, the method of discussion used in the Great Books program. In shared inquiry, participants who have carefully read an assigned work of literature come together to help each other explore the author's meaning. Each participant brings a unique perspective that influences how he or she understands the assigned story or essay; thus, by sharing their interpretations in discussion, participants can discover new aspects of the work and deepen or even change their initial understanding of it.

At the heart of shared inquiry are interpretive questions—questions that address specific problems about the meaning of a work. At the start of discussion, the leader poses a prepared interpretive question to which he or she does not yet have a satisfactory answer, one that the leader is genuinely interested in exploring with the group. As participants begin responding, the leader follows up on what their answers mean, asking questions about how the responses relate to the interpretive question and to other ideas put forward by the group and about how they are supported by and illuminate the text. Throughout shared inquiry, the leader provides guidance only by careful questioning. Because the leader does not provide answers, participants are challenged to think for themselves. By trying out ideas and exchanging and examining opinions, they build their own answers to the interpretive question under discussion, and they develop their own ways of understanding the work. When everyone feels satisfied that the interpretive question has been thoroughly explored, the discussion ends or the leader poses a new question.

In each discussion, participants gain experience in communicating complex ideas, and in supporting, testing, and expanding their own thoughts. Shared inquiry also helps participants develop the habit of reflective thinking. Reflective thinking, wrote the philosopher John Dewey, is disciplined, purposeful thinking: "It involves turning a subject over in the mind and giving it serious and consecutive consideration. It is a process that starts with a problem and moves toward a solution by sifting, relating, and ordering a flow of ideas." In thinking reflectively about an interpretive problem in discussion, participants learn to give full consideration to the ideas of others, to weigh the merits of opposing arguments, and to modify their initial opinions if the evidence demands it.

Because shared inquiry fosters both the flexibility of mind to consider problems from many different angles and the discipline to analyze ideas critically, Great Books participants can acquire the confidence and the intellectual capability to approach many fields of knowledge. By giving participants practice in asking specific questions and actively seeking out answers and in probing and reevaluating ideas, shared inquiry prepares them to be lifelong learners.

The Great Books program also awakens in participants, especially children, a joy in reading and exploring literary works. The stories and essays in each series are specially selected to facilitate shared inquiry discussion and to address the interests and concerns of the readers using that series. By providing students with a way to approach such challenging works successfully, shared inquiry improves reading comprehension, enhances the reading experience, and motivates participants to read. When readers become involved in a story or find an essay's argument compelling, they bring forward their best efforts at understanding. And the reader whose imagination has been fired, whose sympathy for fictional characters has been stirred, is the one best able to think reflectively and articulate ideas about what he or she has read. Both the private experience of reading such works and the shared experience of discussion deepen participants' understanding of themselves and others.

The Basic Leader Training Course and the information in this book can only serve as an introduction to the principles and practice of shared inquiry discussion. Shared inquiry is an art that must be cultivated over time by participants and leaders alike. Participants must be aware that tentative hypotheses and even wrong turns can lead everyone to a greater understanding of the text under consideration—for in shared inquiry many ideas must be pooled before satisfying interpretations can be realized. Similarly, leaders must be patient with their own false starts and wrong turns. Guiding discussion is a challenging pursuit that will gradually become easier as leaders and group members develop their interpretive skills and learn to work in concert.

Course Requirements

THERE ARE two important requirements for your participation in the Basic Leader Training Course. First, you must be committed to leading a Junior or Adult Great Books discussion group using the readings published by the Great Books Foundation. For Junior groups, the administrator responsible must have agreed to purchase the appropriate series of readings or to allow students to purchase their own copies. There is only one exception to the commitment requirement: administrators who will be directly involved in supervising Great Books programs may enroll in the training course, whether or not they plan to lead a group themselves.

Second, you must attend the entire meeting on both days of the course. Each activity in the Basic Leader Training Course is based on activities that precede it, and all work is done in class. Participants who arrive after the course has begun or who miss any other part of it will not be allowed to participate further.

Interpretive questioning p. 4
p. 11 - 12

About This Manual

As YOU BEGIN leading your own Great Books discussion group, we urge you to turn to this manual often. It will guide you through all the stages in the process of shared inquiry—from carefully reading a selection and taking notes, to writing interpretive questions in preparation for discussion, to asking follow-up questions that keep your participants focused on the problem of meaning you have raised. You will also find advice about introducing shared inquiry to your participants, conducting your first meeting, and dealing with practical difficulties that come up in discussion. The final chapter of the manual will provide you with important information about Junior Great Books selections, curriculum objectives, and program organization.

readers come with their own ~~pr~~ varied
prior knowledge; interpretations, attitudes etc.

- no one answers
- some opinions get very strong
BOOK TALKS
- use first session for guidelines

6 Features of discussion try to touch on big issue in story
1. Ask question with more than one possible answer
   Encourage many answers
2. Write down an ~~answer~~ answer before discussion
   - even write question — helps keep on track
   - keep in mind that answers can change
   - form own opinions first
3. Leader only asks questions, no statements ab. text
(4.) Leader asks for supported evidence from text
   readers should look for that also.
5. Do you agree or disagree?
   Listen to other opinions and make own judgements
   consider other points of view
6. What is author trying to say
   what do we get from story

1

EYE CONTACT

Idea - give a bookmark to
use to write notes or unknown
words

Preparing to Lead a Discussion

OVERVIEW

Because shared inquiry should be a process of discovery for both you and your participants, preparing to lead does not mean exploring every possibility of meaning in a selection or mapping out all the territory a discussion could cover. Instead, your aim is to identify three or four main interpretive problems you would like to concentrate on in discussion. In finding the problems of meaning that interest you, you will become more familiar with the work as a whole. This, in turn, will enable you to respond more effectively to ideas that members of your group offer—and to see what in the selection is prompting those ideas. Here are the main steps in preparing for discussion:

1. Read the selection at least twice and take notes to mark interesting passages, indicate insights, ask questions, and comment on the work's structure.

2. From your notes, identify genuine problems of meaning—those that you still find puzzling after two readings and some reflection, and that you can interpret in more than one way based on the text. To address these problems, write as many **interpretive questions** as you can.

3. Sort the interpretive questions you have written into groups of questions that seem to be related to the same problem of meaning. In each group, try to identify one interpretive question that addresses most comprehensively that group's central concern. This type of comprehensive interpretive question is known as a **basic question**. We call a basic question and its group of related questions a **cluster**.

4. If at all possible, "prediscuss" the selection with a colleague to make sure your prepared questions are clear, interesting, and truly interpretive, and that your clusters are coherent.

5. Select one of your clusters for your group to discuss first. Use the basic question of this cluster to initiate discussion. Reserve your other clusters for use after your initial interpretive problem has been thoroughly explored. ❖

DISTINGUISHING INTERPRETIVE QUESTIONS FROM QUESTIONS OF FACT AND EVALUATION

When reading and experiencing a work of literature, we do so on three levels. The first and most fundamental level is that of fact, all the "givens" of a work. In fiction, any information the author provides about the world of the story —every detail of setting, character, and plot—is a "fact," whether or not it corresponds to our perception of reality. For example, in "Jack and the Beanstalk," it is a "fact" that ogres live in the sky. In nonfiction, the author's statements—propositions, lines of argument, conclusions—are "facts." Comprehension and appreciation of the facts of a work lay the foundation for the next level of reading: interpretation.

To interpret a story or essay is to construct explanations of what the author wants us to think about and experience through his or her words. Interpretation begins with the questions that come to us as we read. Why does a character act in a certain way? Why does the author include a particular detail? Why do things turn out as they do? What does a certain word mean in context? As we develop answers to such questions, we get a better sense of how the parts of the work fit together and of what the work means.

The third way we respond to a work of literature is evaluation. When we evaluate a work, we consider its bearing on our lives and its broader implications, even if it poses ideas that seem inconsistent with our own values and personal experience. We judge what the author has written, deciding for ourselves whether it is true. Just as a firm grasp of the facts of a work is essential to thoughtful interpretation, a solid understanding of the author's meaning is the basis for intelligent evaluation.

Corresponding to these three levels of reading are three kinds of questions that are addressed in shared inquiry: questions of fact, interpretation, and evaluation. A **question of fact** has only one correct answer. It asks participants to recall something the author says, and can usually be answered by pointing to a passage in the selection. For example, the answer to the question *What does Jack take from the ogre the first time he goes up the beanstalk?* is explicitly stated in the text: a bag of gold.

Sometimes, however, a question of fact cannot be answered by pointing to any single place in the text; rather, its answer must be inferred from other facts available in the selection. For instance, the answer to the question *Did Jack plan to steal from the ogre when he climbed the beanstalk for the first time?* does not appear explicitly in the story. But we can conclude that since this was Jack's first climb (a fact), he could not have had knowledge of the ogre and so could not have planned to steal from him (reasonable inference). Since this inference represents the only logical conclusion, it takes on the force of a "fact." The question *Does the golden harp want to go with Jack?* is also factual for the same reason: although the answer does not appear explicitly in the text, it can be inferred with reasonable certainty from other evidence that *is* explicit. The fact that the harp cries out for its master is sufficient proof that it does not want to go with Jack.

A **question of interpretation** asks participants to look carefully at what happens in a story and to consider what the story means. Unlike a factual question, an interpretive question has more than one reasonable answer that can be supported with evidence from the text. For example, consider the question *Why does Jack make the third trip to the ogre's house?* Several answers are possible. Jack may have been driven by curiosity or greed to see what else the ogre had in his house. Perhaps he longed for further adventures, or took pleasure in outwitting the ogre. Or Jack may have wanted to prove himself to his mother—or been worried that the hen might stop laying, just as Milky-white had gone dry. The text provides reasonable support for each of these answers. Because the question raises a substantial problem of meaning—one that can be interpreted in more than one way based on evidence in the story—it is capable of sustaining a rewarding discussion.

Questions of evaluation ask us to consider a work in light of our own knowledge, values, or experience of life, to decide whether we agree with what the author has written. Two examples of evaluative questions are: *Is it neces-*

sary to take risks—*as Jack does*—*in order to grow up and be responsible?* and *In your opinion, is the author justified in rewarding Jack?* Participants will be prepared to address the broad issues in these questions only after coming to their own understanding of how Jack behaves and matures throughout the story. If such questions are introduced prematurely, before the meaning of the work has been fully explored, they tend to invite personal ramblings that have little to do with the selection itself.

In shared inquiry discussion, we concentrate on questions of interpretation, referring to the facts of the work for evidence and reserving evaluation for the time when our interpretation is complete. The distinguishing characteristics of factual, interpretive, and evaluative questions are summarized below:

literal
right there
search & find

A factual question has only one correct answer.

An interpretive question has more than one answer that can be supported with evidence from the text.

bring own opinions
and values to the story

on your own

An evaluative question asks us to judge a work, to decide whether we agree with what the author has written. The answer to an evaluative question depends on our own knowledge, experience, and values, as well as on our own interpretation of the work.

use at end of discussion

To put it another way: Questions of fact ask, "What does the author say?" Questions of interpretation ask, "What does the author mean by what he or she says?" Questions of evaluation ask, in light of our interpretation, "Is what the author says and means true?"

ACTIVE READING AND TAKING NOTES

Carefully read the selection twice and take notes.

Your first step in preparing to lead a discussion is to read the selection carefully at least twice, actively noting your reactions to the work. Making notes will lead you to think through what the author says and come to terms with the ideas of the selection in your own way. Noting your responses will also help you develop confidence about your understanding of the selection: by expressing your thoughts—even in scattered marginal comments—you begin to identify those special problems that hold your interest. Notations that address these problems will be the main source of your interpretive questions.

Because Great Books reading selections are rich in ideas, two separate readings are necessary to prepare for discussion. On your first reading, concentrate on getting a sense of the work as a whole. When reading fiction, for example, ask yourself: What are the main stages in the plot? What are the main unifying ideas or problems in the story? Are the actions of the characters consistent and convincing? Do the events in the story seem to make sense in light of my own experience?

When reading nonfiction, you might find it easier to follow an author's argument if you pencil in your own titles for sections, paragraphs, and pages. You might also outline a selection, numbering its major points and noting supporting statements and examples. Rough diagrams or charts can sometimes help you make sense of complex passages. If you find a section of the text particularly difficult, try putting the author's argument into your own words. In addition, note any term that the author seems to use in a special way and trace it throughout the work to understand what it means in different contexts.

Give yourself some time between readings to let your ideas and impressions settle. On your second reading, you may want to concentrate on specific portions of the selection that interest or puzzle you, analyzing them and relating them to the work as a whole. Because you already know the outcome of the story or understand the general thrust of the author's argument, you can more clearly recognize the connections among incidents in the plot or points in the argument. Having the author's "big picture" in mind as you read will also make unusual word choice and recurrent ideas and images more noticeable. Your second reading will let you refine and correct first impressions, answer many of your initial questions, and find some new problems of meaning.

Looking for genuine problems of meaning in the selection, those that *persist* as problems even after careful reflection, is one of the aims of active reading. But often, especially at this stage, you cannot be sure if something is truly puzzling or if it can be easily resolved with a little more thought. For this reason, you should be open-minded and jot down any reactions you have. Be alert to all the possibilities of meaning you see in the selection, and don't be overly concerned with analyzing and assessing your responses. Here are a few note-taking suggestions:

Note anything you do not understand. If a character says or does something that puzzles you, note it in the margin. If you find some aspect of an author's argument unclear, make a note explaining what perplexes you. Chances are what puzzles you will puzzle others as well.

Note anything you think is especially important. For those passages that strike you as particularly significant, try to express exactly why they attract your attention and hold your interest. If you have a question about an essential part of an author's argument, write it in the margin. Note also the connections you perceive between different parts of the selection. If you begin to see a pattern in the author's use of language or in a character's actions, remind yourself to look again at related passages.

Note anything about which you feel strongly. If you disagree with an author's argument, make a note about why you differ. If a character's actions trouble you, explain your response in the margin. Noting your agreement can be equally useful. Passages that cause you to respond strongly, either positively or negatively, will usually provoke a similar reaction in your participants. If your response is undiminished after your second reading, you might want to focus on the passage or problem in discussion.

Some experienced leaders find it helpful to distinguish the notes from their first and second readings. They use different colored pens or different markings, or switch from pen to pencil. Knowing if a note is a first impression or a later consideration can be particularly important as you begin to write discussion questions. The facing page shows the notes a reader took on the beginning of "Jack and the Beanstalk"; the gray notes are from the second reading.

Jack and the Beanstalk

Told by Joseph Jacobs

THERE was once upon a time a poor widow who had an only son named Jack and a cow named Milky-white. And all they had to live on was the milk the cow gave every morning, which they carried to the market and sold. But one morning Milky-white gave no milk and they didn't know what to do.

"What shall we do, what shall we do?" said the widow, wringing her hands.

"Cheer up, mother, I'll go and get work somewhere," said Jack.

"We've tried that before, and nobody would take you," said his mother. "We must sell Milky-white and with the money start a shop or something."

"All right, mother," says Jack. "It's market day today, and I'll soon sell Milky-white, and then we'll see what we can do."

So he took the cow's halter in his hand, and off he started. He hadn't gone far when he met a funny-looking old man who said to him: "Good morning, Jack."

"Good morning to you," said Jack, and wondered how he knew his name.

"Well, Jack, and where are you off to?" said the man.

"I'm going to market to sell our cow here."

"Oh, you look the proper sort of chap to sell cows," said the man. "I wonder if you know how many beans make five."

"Two in each hand and one in your mouth," says Jack, as sharp as a needle.

"Right you are," says the man. "And here they are, the very beans themselves," he went on, pulling out of his pocket a number of strange-looking beans. "As you are so sharp," says he, "I don't mind doing a swap with you—your cow for these beans."

"Go along," says Jack. "Wouldn't you like it?"

"Ah! you don't know what these beans are," said the man. "If you plant them overnight, by morning they grow right up to the sky."

"Really?" says Jack. "You don't say so."

"Yes, that is so, and if it doesn't turn out to be true you can have your cow back."

"Right," says Jack, and hands him over Milky-white's halter and pockets the beans.

Back goes Jack home, and as he hadn't gone very far it wasn't dusk by the time he got to his door.

"Back already, Jack?" said his mother. "I see you haven't got Milky-white, so you've sold her. How much did you get for her?"

"You'll never guess, mother," says Jack.

"No, you don't say so. Good boy! Five pounds, ten, fifteen, no, it can't be twenty."

"I told you you couldn't guess. What do you say to these beans; they're magical, plant them overnight and—"

"What!" says Jack's mother. "Have you been such a fool, such a dolt, such an idiot, as to give away my Milky-white, the best milker in the parish, and prime beef to boot, for a set of paltry beans? Take that! Take that! Take that! And as for your precious beans, here they go out of the window. And now off with you to bed. Not a sip shall you drink, and not a bit shall you swallow this very night."

So Jack went upstairs to his little room in the attic, and sad and sorry he was, to be sure, as much for his mother's sake as for the loss of his supper.

Handwritten marginal notes: desperate situation · Naive? Optimistic? · son? / laws? · Cautious? · flattery · Why not? · Is this silly or clever? · old! · ? sarcasm? or praise · helping or taking advantage? · what makes him decide? Smart? or Foolish? · guarantee!? · man never said this · she plants beans · Cruel

One note from the first reading poses a question about something not understood: "Why does Jack decide to trade the cow for the beans?" Other notes express emotional responses ("cruel mother"); offer judgments about characters' words and actions ("optimistic," "naive," "flattery"); or indicate observations about things that seem important ("The man never exactly tells Jack the beans are magical" and "The mother actually plants the beans").

On the second reading, new sources of puzzlement are noted: "Is Jack's answer to the man a silly or a clever one?" and "What good is the guarantee?" Earlier notes are reconsidered and some guesses are made about their meaning: "Does the man's flattery mean he is trying to take advantage of Jack?" and "Is Jack clever or foolish to trade his cow for five beans?" Some details not noted before are now seen as important: "Is 'sharp as a needle' praise or sarcasm?" and "Why does the author make the mother a widow?"

WRITING INTERPRETIVE QUESTIONS

From your notes, write as many interpretive questions as you can to address problems of meaning in the selection.

Leading a Great Books discussion calls for a balance between planning and spontaneity. In preparation, you want to become familiar enough with a selection so that you will be able to respond helpfully to the ideas and insights that your participants bring up. You also want to know the work well enough to be able to guide your participants to passages in the text that are relevant to their ideas—and to your questions. On the other hand, you do not want to prepare in such a way that you get stuck on one interpretation of the story and find yourself asking leading questions meant to get across a single point of view.

The best way to achieve this "planned spontaneity" is to keep an open mind about a selection and write as many interpretive questions as you can. The process of writing and revising questions will lead you to grapple with, and form preliminary ideas about, a work's most important interpretive problems. Many experienced leaders will write thirty or forty questions as they consider and reconsider the problems of meaning in a selection. Many of these initial interpretive questions will be dropped for various reasons; others will be revised. But the more you have, the easier it will be to compile a list of twelve or so that are especially thought-provoking and important, and the freer you will be to discard those that are less interesting or significant. And each question you think about will increase your understanding of the selection and make you better prepared to follow up on the thoughts of your participants.

Generating Interpretive Questions from Your Notes

Many questions will come to you easily as you read, and others will occur to you right after you finish a selection, when your mind is first wrestling with the entire work. Later, more deliberate reflection about the selection will help you produce new questions. As you look back over the work, think again about interesting passages and review your notes carefully. Some of the notations you made may no longer seem significant, but others will suggest ideas that continue to hold your interest. Notes that address the following are especially good sources for questions:

Character motivation. Look for notes that question the reasons behind a character's statements, actions, or thoughts. For example, the author of "Jack and the Beanstalk" writes that Jack climbed the beanstalk the third time because he was "not content," but why does Jack feel this way? Does he want more gold—or does he long for more adventure? Your doubt about Jack's motives could lead to the interpretive question *Why does Jack climb the beanstalk the third time?*

Striking or unusual use of language. Some of your notes may indicate surprise at the way an author expresses an idea or casts a description. For example, thinking about Jack's reply to the funny-looking old man might lead you to ask this question: *Why does the author have Jack answer the old man's question by saying, "Two in each hand and one in your mouth"?* Does Jack's answer suggest immaturity—or a quick wit? Or does his answer indicate that Jack is naturally acquisitive, that he thinks in terms of consuming as much as he can?

Prominent details. Although you won't want to question the purpose of every detail, some details can function as important elements in an interpretation. Consider the question *Why does the author make Jack's mother a poor widow?* Does it seem significant to you that Jack is poor and fatherless? What bearing does this information have on our understanding of Jack's adventures? Expressing your doubt about how to interpret a detail that you noted can lead your group to a fresh understanding of a story or essay.

Words, phrases, or sentences that can be understood in more than one way. Often, the way a word or phrase is used will attract your attention and cause you to consider if it has special significance. If examining the context of the word or phrase doesn't help you pinpoint a definite interpretation—and, in the case of a puzzling word, if a dictionary does not seem to settle the matter—then write a question that calls attention to the ambiguity you find. For example, doubt about the tone of the author's comment that Jack was "as sharp as a needle" might lead you to ask, *Is the author sarcastic when he writes that Jack was "as sharp as a needle" in responding to the old man?*

Connections between passages, characters, incidents, or ideas. The various parts of a well-crafted work of literature are interconnected; they support one another. Discovering the meaning of a story or essay depends on understanding the relationships between its parts. In "Jack and the Beanstalk," Jack's three adventures in the sky are similar in many respects—the climb, the theft, the escape—but their parallelism also serves to highlight significant differences. Noting that on his second trip Jack confronts the ogre's wife in a more assured manner, you could ask, *Why is Jack so much bolder in asking the ogre's wife for food on his second trip than he had been on his first?* Is he just hungry, as he was before? Is he gaining time to look around? Is he braver—or is he being foolhardy? In this case, comparing parallel scenes can spotlight Jack's developing confidence and cleverness as well as the wife's changing role. Other examples are *Why does the author have the ogre's wife give Jack breakfast, whereas his own mother deprives him of food?* or *Why does the author have Jack take a bag of gold, a magic hen, and a golden harp in that order?*

Reviewing your notes is an excellent way to generate interpretive questions, but another important source is your thoughtful consideration of what the entire work seems to mean. After reading a selection a second time, go over passages that seem especially significant or striking, such as those dealing with a moment of crisis or a decisive change in a character. Then step back and ask yourself what, in broad terms, are the work's major themes and ideas? For instance, thinking about the changes Jack undergoes in the course of his adventures could lead you to ask, *Why do Jack's adventures enable him to grow up successfully in the story?* Often, considering a more comprehensive problem of meaning will change the focus of other questions and bring new interpretive issues to mind.

What Makes a Good Interpretive Question?

When you ask a question to start discussion, in effect you are saying, "Here is a place in the text that suggests something important to me, but I'm having trouble deciding what it means, what its significance is. With your help, I would like to think more about this problem." You want your participants to be able to respond—and to *want* to respond—when they hear your initial question. You want them to understand right away what you are asking and to be able to think about what details in the selection bear on the problem you have raised. What makes a good interpretive question, one that can get your participants interested immediately? Here are the main characteristics:

You should have genuine doubt about the answer or answers to the question. Doubt does not mean, "I know the best answer, but my participants may not." Doubt means that after identifying and considering a problem of meaning, you are still unsure about how to resolve it. The problem *persists,* and so you want to share the question with your group to find out what they think about it.

To check whether you have doubt about a question, try to write at least two different answers and support each with evidence from the selection. If the text seems to provide reasonable support for at least two answers, and you're not sure which you prefer, then for you that question raises a point about which you have doubt. It would be difficult to have doubt about the answer to *Is Scho as good a ball player as Glennie and Monk?* because the text strongly suggests that the answer is "no." Likewise, *Do Monk and Glennie try to exclude Scho from their game?* is not suitable for discussion because it has only one reasonable answer based on the evidence in the story.

"Leading questions," questions meant to lead your participants to a single answer that you think is important, are also unsuitable for shared inquiry. You cannot have doubt about the answer to a leading question because you have already decided what the "correct" response should be. For example, the question *Don't you think the title "A Game of Catch" refers to more than Monk and Glennie's game?* tends to push participants to respond with a "yes." Similarly, *Do you really think Scho fell from the tree deliberately?* seems with the term "really" to betray the leader's lack of doubt about the question.

You should care about the question. Write questions about interpretive problems that really interest you; concentrate on problems that you feel are important. Your enthusiasm for a question can be contagious, leading to a lively exchange of ideas among the members of your group. If you ask a question you don't care about, your participants will sense your lack of interest and respond superficially with whatever they imagine will quickly bring discussion to a close.

Your question should be discussible. Does the question send you to the selection for answers? And does the selection contain the evidence needed to support answers? Sometimes, a work captures us so thoroughly we lose track of the limits of the world that the author has created. The question *How will Glennie and Monk react the next time they are playing catch and Scho comes along?* inquires about a period of time not encompassed by the selection, and so involves speculating beyond the facts of the story. Also speculative are questions that ask what would have happened had events in the work been different, as in this example: *Would Glennie and Monk have walked away if Scho hadn't fallen from the tree?* Finally, some questions about specific details, such as *Why doesn't Scho have a glove?* and *How old is Scho?* are not discussible because answers cannot be supported with evidence from the text. Unlike a good interpretive question, all these questions will fail to keep participants grounded in the text and moving toward a fuller understanding of the story.

Your question should be clear. An interpretive question should be easy for your participants to understand; otherwise, they will have to spend valuable discussion time in simply trying to figure out what the question means. Consider how your participants would respond to the unnecessarily difficult language of this question: *Does Scho exhibit symptoms of delusion in his verbal attempts to control Glennie and Monk?* A question that is poorly focused will also seem unclear: *Why does the author have Scho climb up to what he calls a "wonderful seat," and which the author later calls a "cradle of slight branches"?* Both of these questions would stump most participants. In writing questions, strive for a clarity and sharpness that will prompt your group to begin thinking of answers right away.

Your question should be specific. If a question can be applied to many other selections with only a few word changes, it is probably too general. *What is Scho's attitude toward Monk and Glennie?* and *What does Scho's game represent?* are examples of overly broad questions that could easily be altered for use with other stories. Such questions do not give participants a definite problem to explore; nor will they spark the interest of your group. To bring the problem you want to consider into focus and to avoid getting vague responses, make your questions as specific to the selection as you can.

Revising Your Interpretive Questions

Many of the interpretive questions you write will need to be reworked. Some of your questions will turn out to be factual, evaluative, or unclear. Or you may find that several weaker questions can evolve into a single one that better expresses a particular problem. Sometimes, you'll write several versions of the same question, refining it until it best conveys what you want your group to consider. Deciding which formulation of a question is best involves your estimation of what will get your participants to react. While there are no rules for transforming your initial questions into ones that are sharply focused and provocative, the following suggestions will help you in making your revisions:

Revising factual questions. If a question turns out to be factual, or if you eventually come to lack doubt about it, check to see if its answer will lead you to an interpretive question. For example, your initial thinking about "A Game of Catch" might lead you to ask, *Does Scho play a game of his own?* The answer to this question—that Scho does indeed play his own game in pretending to control Glennie and Monk—suggests the revised question *Why does Scho pretend he can control Glennie and Monk?* This revision, unlike the original, has a number of different answers because it explores Scho's motives for playing his game. Similarly, *Why does Scho fall from the tree?* might seem factual to you if you feel certain that Scho's fall was a deliberate part of his game. One possible revision can make use of your answer: *Why does Scho deliberately fall from the tree?*

If you come to lack doubt about the answer to a question, try revising it to include a reasonable assumption. Suppose that in thinking about the question *Does Scho remain an outsider throughout the story?* you eventually conclude that for you the answer is "yes." Instead of discarding the question, change its focus by making use of your assumption that Scho does indeed remain an outsider: *Why does Scho remain an outsider throughout the story?* Other examples of questions that incorporate assumptions are: *Why can't Scho participate in Monk and Glennie's game of catch?* and *Why does Scho feel more powerful in the tree than he does on the ground?* If the assumption is shared by everyone, it serves as an appropriate point for the discussion to begin. If participants challenge your assumption—if, for instance, someone doubts that Scho can't participate in the game, or that he felt more powerful in the tree—then opposing viewpoints will be discussed as all opinions are discussed in shared inquiry, weighed against the evidence in the text.

Revising evaluative questions. If a question on your list is evaluative, try rewording it so that instead of calling for a judgment it asks about a problem of meaning in the text. You could revise the question *Why would someone try to join a game that is proceeding so beautifully without him?* to ask *Why does Scho want to be included in the game of catch?* The former question asks that participants judge Scho's behavior; the revision encourages them to discuss his motivation using evidence from the story.

Making vocabulary clear. Some questions might be hard for your group to answer because of difficult vocabulary, jargon, or technical terms. The question *Is it ego gratification that makes Scho play his game?* assumes that your participants have a knowledge of psychology. But the revision *Why does Scho pretend he can control Glennie and Monk?* addresses the problem of Scho's motivation in simpler terms suggested by the text. Sometimes, apparently simple but abstract words like "evil" or "good" can be more troublesome than technical terms and unfamiliar vocabulary. A question like *Are we to conclude that Scho is wicked at heart?* would probably result in a semantic tug-of-war between participants who have different ideas of what "wicked at heart" means. Instead, direct your participants to a specific incident in the text that made you think of the problem in the first place. Ask, for instance, *Why does Scho persist in his game even after Glennie invites him to come down and play catch?*

Making vague questions specific. Participants might also be baffled about how to respond to a question that is too general. Instead of asking *What causes Scho to have such mixed feelings at the end of the story?*, try to use the author's own language to make the problem clearer: *Why does Scho have feelings of both "triumph" and "misery" at the end of the story?* Similarly, the question *What is Scho's attitude toward Monk and Glennie?* does not give participants enough information about the problem you want them to consider. Scho's attitude toward the boys, which changes in the course of the story, would be better explored through more specific questions, such as *Why does Scho say he can make Glennie and Monk do whatever he wants?* and *Why doesn't Scho accept Glennie's invitation to come down from the tree and play catch?* General questions about what something "represents" or "symbolizes" should also be revised. Instead of *What does the tree symbolize?*, ask more specific questions such as *Why does the author have Scho climb a tree?* or *Why does the author have Scho play his game in a tree?*

Identifying issues in your questions. Be alert to interpretive problems that require a choice between two plausible answers that are in especially strong opposition. If you have genuine doubt about which of the answers is preferable, then instead of leaving the question open, state the alternatives for your participants to weigh. For example, the question *Why does Glennie ask Scho if he has his glove, when it's obvious that he doesn't?* could be revised this way: *Is Glennie's question "Got your glove?" an invitation for Scho to play, or a way of dismissing him?* Identifying an issue for your group can make discussion more interesting because participants will have to take a stand and choose between competing points of view. Be certain, though, that the alternatives you offer in the question are the ones most strongly suggested by the selection. If several other answers are equally plausible, your question will end up restricting inquiry.

Rethinking questions that include the author. Some of your questions will ask about the author's attitude toward the characters, reasons for including specific details, or purpose in writing the story. In reviewing such questions, consider whether you should shift the focus from the author to the characters. For example, the question *Why does the author have Scho continue his game after Monk apologizes to him?* will force your group to think about Scho from an unnecessarily abstract perspective. By asking instead, *Why does Scho continue his game after Monk apologizes to him?,* you will get your participants to explore Scho's motives and feelings more directly.

On the other hand, the question *Why are Glennie and Monk so good at their game?* is less suited for shared inquiry than *Why does the author make Glennie and Monk so good at their game?* The first question would elicit only speculative answers—perhaps the boys were naturally athletic or played together often—which would not lead participants to a greater understanding of the story. The second question, however, raises the larger—and more discussible—matter of why Glennie and Monk's skill is important in the story.

Many interpretive issues can be phrased as either a problem of character motivation or a problem of the author's intention. However, the addition of "the author" to a question like *Why does Scho climb the tree?* will alter the type of answers you hear in discussion. Do you want your participants to talk about Scho's reasons for climbing the tree—or the author's reasons for having him do it? In a case like this, be sure to use the form of the question that reflects the problem you want your group to explore.

Revising interpretive questions is not a science. The phrasing you choose represents your best judgment about what will most clearly convey an interpretive problem as you see it and what will most effectively get your participants involved. Consider the following variations on a question that appears above as well as in the Leader Aid for Series Six:

> Why does Scho pretend he controls Glennie and Monk?

> Does Scho pretend he controls Glennie and Monk because he wants to disrupt their game or because he wants to be included?

> Why does Scho play a game that disrupts Glennie and Monk's game of catch?

> Does Scho disrupt Glennie and Monk's game out of spite or because he wants to be included?

Although each of these questions has a slightly different focus, they all concern Scho's motivation for playing his game—and they would all be suitable for discussion. When improving your interpretive questions, keep in mind that there is no such thing as the "perfect" wording. Refining ideas—including your own—is part of the process of shared inquiry. In discussion, you should be flexible about your questions and ready to rephrase them if your participants are having a hard time responding.

GROUPING YOUR PREPARED INTERPRETIVE QUESTIONS: BASIC QUESTIONS AND CLUSTERS

> *Sort your interpretive questions into clusters and select a basic question to serve as the focus of discussion.*

After writing your interpretive questions, you need to think about how you'll be using them in discussion. Which questions address major problems and themes? Which probe more specific details? What are the relationships among the questions? To get a handle on the relative importance of each question, and to put into sharper perspective the larger, more comprehensive problems of meaning suggested by the work, you should sort your questions into groups.

Grouping your interpretive questions involves putting together those questions that bear on the same problem for interpretation and then identifying—or writing—a **basic question** for each group. A basic question is one that addresses in a comprehensive way a central problem of meaning in the selection; answering a basic question satisfactorily requires the examination of many passages in the text. A **cluster** is a group of interpretive questions that are all related to a single basic question. The questions in a cluster might approach the problem in the basic question from different perspectives, address separate parts of the problem, or examine various pieces of evidence that bear on the problem.

Working on "A Game of Catch," a leader might develop a cluster that looks something like this:

> ***Basic Question:*** According to the author, do Glennie and Monk treat Scho unfairly?
>
> Is Glennie's question "Got your glove?" an invitation for Scho to play, or a way of dismissing him?
>
> Why does Glennie invite Scho down from the tree to play catch?
>
> Why does Monk apologize for causing Scho's fall from the tree?
>
> Why does Monk begin to throw the ball to Glennie once or twice before he gives Scho the hard, bumpy grounder?

The basic question, which looks into the behavior of Glennie and Monk with respect to Scho, addresses a central problem of understanding the way the characters interact. Each question in the cluster refers to a point in the story when the motives of Glennie or Monk are in doubt: Glennie's ambiguous question, "Got your glove?"; his suggestion that Scho climb down from the tree; Monk's apology; and his hard throw to Scho. These questions thus direct attention to evidence that is relevant to answering the basic question. Rather than arranging the questions chronologically, the leader pairs off questions probing Glennie's motives, and those examining Monk's. A different order might make more sense to you.

In shared inquiry, asking a number of related questions—rather than an assortment of unrelated ones—will make your group's exploration of the selection more thorough and coherent. But a cluster is only a provisional plan for helping your participants resolve the comprehensive interpretive problem posed by your basic question. Discussion itself will determine which questions from the cluster you'll use, and when to use them. For more on how to use questions from a prepared cluster in discussion, turn to page 31.

If you have a coleader or colleague to work with, write questions independently and then meet to go over them and to develop clusters. If you are working alone, preparing clusters will help you explore the selection more fully on your own. Here's how to prepare clusters from your list of interpretive questions:

1. Separate your interpretive questions. Writing each question on a separate index card or slip of paper will enable you to move questions around as you consider how they are related.

2. Group your questions, placing together those that seem to deal with the same problem of meaning. When you are finished, you should have three or four piles, each containing several questions that concern an interpretive problem you wish to explore. To test whether a question belongs in a given cluster, begin to answer it; the answers you get will help you determine if the question is related to others in the group. Some questions will not seem to fit with any of the others; put these aside.

3. Select or write a basic interpretive question for each cluster. Examine each group to determine whether it contains a question that states the problem in a comprehensive fashion. If no question in the group seems "basic," write an interpretive question to cover the main issue the cluster addresses.

4. Develop the clusters. Consider whether any of the questions you have put aside can be revised and included in a cluster. (If not, consider whether one or more of these questions can form the beginning of another group.) Write additional questions to fill out the clusters as necessary—you should have four or five questions in each cluster. Check to see whether the answers to each question in a cluster will help you answer the basic question. If two questions bring up similar answers, discard the question that seems less clear. If a question is only a close restatement of the basic question, drop it or revise it.

5. Arrange the questions in each cluster in an order that makes sense to you.

After working with your questions and grouping them, you will find that some of your clusters address problems that seem more comprehensive, more essential to the meaning of the work, or just more interesting to you. Select one of these clusters for your group to discuss first. It is the basic question from this cluster that you will use to initiate discussion. Keep the other clusters on hand; having basic questions in reserve will let you go on to a new problem after your initial one has been satisfactorily explored.

PREDISCUSSION

In prediscussion, go over your questions with a colleague who has read the selection.

If you have a coleader, you should always meet with him or her sometime before your discussion to review your prepared interpretive questions. If you have no coleader, it is an excellent idea to meet with a colleague who has agreed to read the selection. This "prediscussion" gives you the opportunity to share your thinking about a selection, refine your questions, generate new ones, and develop clusters. It is also the best way to try out your questions to decide which ones you will ask your group. Working with a partner will make your preparation more enjoyable; it will also make you a more confident leader.

When you meet, bring along all your notes and the questions you have written. Test your questions on each other, checking to see whether they might be answered in more than one way based on the selection. Keep track of where you find relevant evidence in the text; later, during discussion, the page numbers you have jotted down will make it easier to direct participants to important passages. If the two of you strongly disagree about how to answer a question, it is often an excellent one to ask your group. Also, exploring differences between your interpretations will sometimes help you come up with new and more interesting questions.

As you go through your questions, continue to rethink and improve them. Put aside any factual or evaluative questions and those that turn out to be weak duplicates of others. Then select your best questions and check them to make sure they are clear, specific, and thought-provoking. Sort the questions into clusters, following the steps suggested earlier in this section. Finally, choose the cluster that you will use to start discussion.

Distance often improves judgment, so try to let a few days pass between the writing of your questions and your review of them—especially if there is no one with whom you can prepare. You might also want to compare your questions to those published in the Leader Aid for that series (see p. 51). The Aid questions can supplement your thinking, serving as a second point of view, when you are ready to decide which questions you want to ask in discussion. ❖

2

Leading
a Discussion

OVERVIEW

Shared inquiry begins when you ask your group a basic question that will serve as the focus of discussion. During discussion, participants exchange their ideas freely, but within the framework of **four rules** that make shared inquiry a disciplined activity. These four rules, along with the **suggestions for starting discussion** and the **discussion guidelines** described in this chapter, will help you create the kind of environment that promotes good habits of reading, thinking, listening, and speaking.

As leader, your aim is to elicit your participants' ideas and opinions about your basic question. You want to help them share, test, and clarify their thinking and, ultimately, to resolve the problem of meaning you have posed. You do all this by asking **follow-up questions.** A few of your follow-up questions will come from the clusters of interpretive questions you developed while preparing for discussion. But most will be your on-the-spot responses to your participants' comments. Follow-up questions will allow you to clarify responses; to ask for evidence in support of opinions; to pursue especially intriguing answers; and to invite new responses to your question.

When you feel the basic question has been thoroughly examined, you have reached a point of **resolution.** Before going on to a new question, try to uncover any answers to the basic question that have not yet been offered in discussion and encourage participants to determine whether each of them has arrived at a satisfactory answer. Then, if you have more time, ask your group another basic question to begin discussion of a new topic. ❖

THE FOUR RULES OF SHARED INQUIRY

Observe the four rules that regulate discussion.

In shared inquiry, the freedom that participants have to express their opinions is regulated by four rules that stipulate who should participate, what is discussed, how opinions are judged, and how discussion is led:

Only those who have read the selection may take part in discussion. Participants who have not read the selection cannot support their opinions with evidence from the text or make sound judgments about what others say about the work.

Discussion is restricted to the selection that everyone has read. This rule gives everyone an equal chance to contribute because it limits discussion to a selection that all participants are familiar with and have before them. When the selection is the sole focus of discussion, everyone can determine whether facts are accurately recalled and opinions adequately supported.

All opinions should be supportable with evidence from the selection. Participants may introduce outside opinions only if they can restate the opinions in their own words and support the ideas with evidence from the selection. Making sure that participants support their ideas with evidence from the text encourages more careful reading.

Leaders may only ask questions—they may not answer them. Your job as leader is to help yourself and your participants understand a selection by asking questions that prompt thoughtful inquiry. If participants get the impression that you have "the" correct answer, they will look for you to supply it instead of developing their own interpretations.

Observing the four rules of shared inquiry helps you and your participants make the best possible use of your discussion time. Rule 1 ensures that participants have the opportunity to offer informed opinions about the reading under discussion. Rules 2 and 3 reinforce participants' comprehension and recall of the selection and set the standard for how opinions are weighed. They also encourage participants to think independently by keeping discussion free of specialized knowledge or outside expertise. Rule 4 gives participants the responsibility for developing and expressing their own ideas. By exercising this responsibility together with the other members of the group, participants learn to value their own thinking and to respect the thoughts of others.

Basic Question can always be changed or altered (handwritten annotation)

size 10-12 — more opinions
large group 20-25
—have a recorder
—make 2 smaller groups w/ 2 questions (handwritten annotations)

OPENING THE DISCUSSION

To begin, make up a seating chart on which you can write comments; then open discussion by asking a basic question selected from the interpretive questions you have written.

When your group meets, first make sure that your participants have read the selection carefully at least twice. In reading the selection and taking notes, participants should prepare as you do, and for the same reasons. (See p. 43, "Helping Your Participants Prepare for Discussion.") Then, to begin, make up a **seating chart** and open discussion by asking your basic question. Write your question at the top of the chart.

save charts to see growth — Keeps track of participation — increase in progress (handwritten annotations)

—using a chart helps slow down discussion — guarantees thinking (handwritten annotations)

Making Up a Seating Chart

A seating chart is a useful tool for keeping track of participants' ideas and comments during discussion. Here is what a seating chart might look like in the middle of a discussion of the basic question *Why does Jack climb the beanstalk the third time?*:

Basic Question: Why does Jack climb the beanstalk the third time?

(Seating chart with participants: Lisa, Mary, Peggy, Frank, Tim, Sam, Toby, Mike, Bill, Jennifer, Sally, Leader 1, Leader 2, Tony, Laura, Don, Cathy, Roberta. Comments: Jack/adventure, A Thief, Risk taker, Jack Bored, Jack greedy, Jack wants his mother's approval, Stealing from an Ogre, disagreement, agrees)

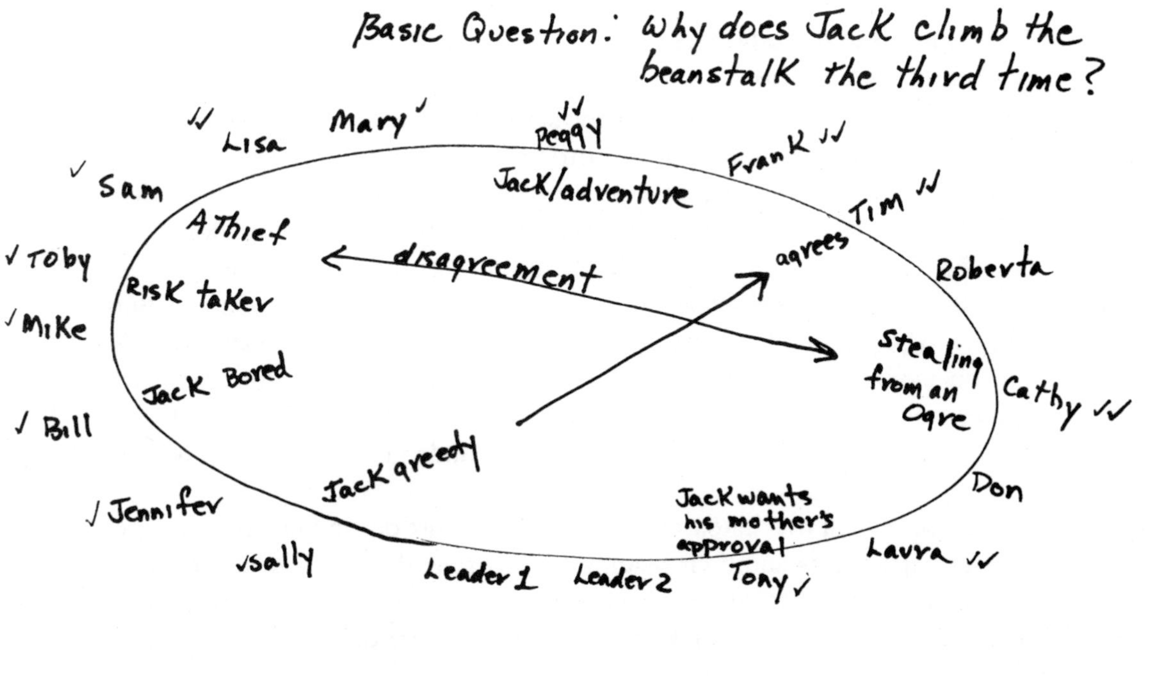

Jot down participants' comments next to their names. Keep your notations short; all you usually need is a word or phrase to indicate important ideas. Lines drawn between names can highlight opinions that are similar or in conflict. Although writing down participants' ideas may take some time, slowing the pace of discussion is often desirable. It gives participants a chance to think about their answers and make connections between related ideas, and it gives you time to think of follow-up questions that make use of your group's comments.

Making up a chart at the start of discussion will enable you to call on each participant by name. If you address questions to the group as a whole, those who like to talk will always respond first and others might not participate at all. Or several people may start talking at the same time. Prefacing each question with someone's name will alert the individual and give him or her time to focus on your question. It will also direct the rest of the participants' attention to that person. You can use your chart to keep a record of individual participation by putting a check mark by a participant's name each time he or she speaks. Then you can call on participants who talk less often to get them involved.

For more about how a seating chart can help you manage the flow of ideas in discussion, turn to page 26.

Recording Initial Responses
to Your Basic Question

After asking your basic question at the start of discussion, have your participants write down the question and record their initial answers. Then, after a few minutes or when everyone seems ready, repeat the question and ask one participant, by name, to give his or her answer. Having participants write down the basic question makes them pay close attention to its specific wording; getting them to record their preliminary answers helps them collect their thoughts. But be sure to emphasize that these early answers are merely a springboard for discussion and by no means should participants feel they must remain committed to their initial ideas. On the contrary, having a record of their first thoughts lets members of the group see how opinions often undergo revision when people share their thinking.

You might want to add to or modify this procedure depending upon the age of your participants and their reading and writing abilities. If your group is composed of younger children or includes students reading below grade level, you or another adult could take a few minutes before discussion to read the selection aloud. If your participants are fluent readers and the selection is short, have your participants read it aloud, round-robin fashion, right before discussion begins. (You might also want to include a reading of the selection at the start of discussion if you find that many of your students have not prepared.) If participants' writing skills are undeveloped, rather than ask students to write down your opening question, you might want to distribute copies of it beforehand. In short, use your judgment to eliminate needless frustrations that might distract your participants from their main task—communicating their ideas about a story in response to your basic question.

CONDUCTING DISCUSSION

Follow discussion guidelines, and conduct discussion by asking questions that follow up on your participants' ideas.

To lead successfully, you need to be involved with the ideas and opinions your participants express. Throughout discussion, you must assess each comment; follow up comments with questions that further discussion; and keep the group moving toward the resolution of your basic question. Here are some general guidelines that will help you accomplish these goals:

Lead slowly. Participants need time to consider the ideas that come up in discussion. If you lead too quickly, calling for new opinions before ideas have been fully clarified or explored, many of your participants will offer inadequate or irrelevant answers or will not respond at all. There are several ways you can keep discussion from moving too fast. Pause for a few seconds after asking a question; when participants answer, help them clarify their responses before you move on. If someone missed a comment, ask the participant who offered the idea to repeat it. Check frequently to see if others understand what is being said. Take the time to frame a follow-up question carefully or to rephrase one that does not seem to be clear to your participants. Let the group hear you think out loud. Taking notes and referring to the comments on your seating chart will also slow the pace of discussion.

Listen carefully to your participants' comments. Try not to be so concerned about what to ask next that you miss what is being said. Your participants' ideas—together with your own thorough preparation—are your best source of follow-up questions. Pay close attention to the wording of comments; the exact phrasing your participants use might suggest subtle differences of opinion or new ways to relate one comment to another. Listening intently also sends a message to your participants that their thoughts are valuable.

Use your seating chart regularly to note ideas. Jotting down the comments that you want to pursue immediately, as well as those you decide to table until later, keeps good ideas from getting lost and lets you give recognition to the participants who initiated them. By keeping track of who said what, you can ask, for example, "Roberta, why do you disagree with what Lisa said before, that Jack is a thief?" Or, "So, Peggy, are you agreeing with Bill that Jack climbs

---

Leading Discussion: Ten Effective Practices

Lead slowly.

Listen carefully.

Use your seating chart regularly.

Encourage participants to talk to one another.

Strive for answers.

Relate ideas to each other and to the basic question.

Turn to the text frequently.

Encourage challenges to assumptions in your questions.

Get everyone to contribute.

Ask follow-up questions often.

---

up again because he's bored?" When participants hear names attached to ideas and opinions, they begin to listen to each other and use each other's thinking to build interpretations. Displaying your filled-out chart when discussion is over will help make your group aware of how their comments contributed to a fuller understanding of a selection.

Encourage participants to talk to one another. In shared inquiry discussion, participants broaden their individual interpretations of a text by exchanging ideas about its meaning. Encourage this exchange by getting participants to ask each other questions and to answer each other directly, rather than through you. Say, "Donna, could you tell Bill why you disagree with his point that...?" Or, "Bill, would you explain to Donna why you think differently?" In this way, you reinforce participants' responsibility for the content and success of discussion, and you emphasize your own role as a fellow inquirer.

Strive for answers. Many times participants do not say exactly what they mean, or they offer what appear to be superficial comments. Striving for answers involves asking one or more follow-up questions to help participants articulate their ideas more clearly. You also want to be persistent about getting your group to find satisfactory answers to your basic question. Stay with a basic question until you believe it has been fully explored. Ask follow-up questions that help your participants relate their current thinking to the basic question: "Tom, can you explain how your idea that Jack is greedy helps us answer the opening question?" Keep everyone on track by occasionally repeating the basic question. If you leave a basic question too soon, be willing to return to it if someone indicates there is more to say.

Relate ideas to each other and to the basic question. Give your discussion continuity and coherence by asking questions that help your participants see the relationships among ideas. Use your seating chart to highlight possible connections between opinions your participants have expressed. Ask, "Jamie, is what you just said different from what Bill said, that...?" Or, "Carla, do you agree with Jamie's point that...or Bill's idea that...?" Let your group see you thinking out loud about the relationships you notice.

Turn to the text frequently. Make a habit of getting participants to locate and read aloud passages that support what they say. Ask, "John, where is that line in the story about Jack's not being content?" Or, "Tom, what in the story made you think that Jack likes adventure? Where was that?" Going back frequently to the text helps participants pick up details that they may have forgotten, or that they missed during their own reading. It also gives everyone a chance to check opinions offered in discussion against the evidence in the selection. (For information on how to help your group analyze a passage in the text in detail, see page 48.)

Encourage participants to challenge any assumptions in your questions. You are free to incorporate reasonable assumptions in your interpretive questions, but your participants are also free to object to them. Your assumption may involve an interpretation that some participants do not agree with or may not yet see for themselves. Consider this a useful opportunity: If a participant seems uncomfortable with a question, ask why. Sorting out the reasons for your disagreement will help clarify the problem to be discussed.

Make sure everyone has an opportunity to contribute. Try to call on each participant several times. Marking your seating chart when someone speaks will help you keep track of participation. Do not let a few articulate students dominate discussion; make it a point to address questions to those who speak rarely or not at all. In time, shy students can become eager participants if you make a gentle but persistent effort to draw them out.

Ask follow-up questions often. Aside from poor preparation, the main reason discussion loses its focus is that leaders fail to ask enough follow-up questions. Follow-up questions are your "contact" with your group. Your spontaneous questioning keeps participants attentive to the central problem and helps them refine their answers. It is through your careful questioning that you and your participants come to understand the selection better.

Using Follow-up Questions *base question on reader's response*

To come up with an appropriate follow-up question, listen to what the participant is saying and think it through. Is the participant's idea clear? Is it relevant? Does it need to be supported with evidence from the selection? Are others in the group likely to understand it? Does it have implications for your basic question? Asking yourself these kinds of questions will help you determine what follow-up question to use. Consider this exchange:

> *Leader:* Mike, why does Jack trade the cow for the beans?
>
> *Mike:* I think that he wants to get away from his mother.
>
> *Leader:* What in the story makes you think he wants to get away from his mother?

Here the leader has asked Mike to support his answer with evidence from the selection. Another appropriate follow-up might be to request clarification: "What do you mean when you say Jack wants to 'get away'?" Or the leader might pursue an implication in Mike's comment: "Does Jack resent the way his mother treats him?" The leader can choose the question that seems best in the context of the discussion, perhaps returning to a second follow-up question later.

Eye Contact

Follow-up questions don't have to be perfectly worded. If your question isn't clear, your participants will let you know, and you can then rephrase it or try another. Take your time in thinking of questions, and concentrate on what your participants are saying. You don't have to follow up on every idea; experienced leaders generally ask one follow-up question for every two or three of their participants' responses. The important thing is to develop a habit of listening carefully and following up with questions.

Here are the most common uses of follow-up questions in discussion:

To clarify comments. Much of what your participants say may need clarification; they need time—and your help—to formulate their responses clearly. If you do not understand a comment or if you notice puzzled looks, then ask the speaker to elaborate on the initial statement or to repeat it in different words: "Martha, what do you mean when you say Jack needs adventure?" Question any special use of language, especially clichés or slang that some members of the group may not be familiar with. This effort to clarify is essential to good discussion, and your participants will gradually grow to feel comfortable with it. They will come to understand that you want to clarify their ideas because you are genuinely interested in exploring them.

To substantiate opinions. Not all opinions offered during your discussion will be equally valid. Some opinions will be better substantiated by evidence from the selection than others. By asking participants to recall or read relevant passages that support what they say, you encourage more attentive reading and help ensure that discussion is tied closely to the text. Thus, if a participant asserts that "Jack is greedy," you might ask, "What in the story makes you think that Jack is greedy, Sarah?" Often you will want to ask how or why the evidence supports the participant's opinion. If Sarah answered, "It says here, 'Jack was not content,' " you might ask, "Why does 'not content' make you think Jack was greedy?"

To solicit additional opinions. Get your participants involved by asking them whether they agree or disagree with a comment under consideration. Ask, "John, do you agree with Mary's point that...?" or "Bill, how would you answer the question I just asked Sylvia?" Then follow up on the answers they give. Participants may offer the same opinion but have different reasons and different evidence for it. Such differences may indicate new avenues for exploring the selection.

When you ask participants for additional opinions, your task is not merely to add them mechanically to the discussion; you want to try to build relationships among the new ideas and those already offered. After a new idea has been explained, try to ask a question to link it back to earlier comments: "Andrea, is your idea that Jack climbed up the third time to get more money different from Jeff's idea that Jack just wanted to take care of his mother?"

To develop an idea by pursuing its implications. Your participants may fail to see all the consequences of their own thinking. If you feel that an idea expressed in discussion has important implications, use a follow-up question to draw them out. In the following exchange, the leader is making an effort to get at the train of thought behind an interpretation:

> *Leader:* Tony, why does Jack climb the beanstalk the third time?
>
> *Tony:* He's greedy. On the second trip, he gets the hen that lays golden eggs. He wouldn't have to climb the stalk as long as the hen lived.
>
> *Leader:* Does having the hen make him greedy?

By pursuing the implications of what your participants say, you help them enlarge and clarify their opinions. And, in the process, you uncover more ideas for your group to consider.

To test whether an idea is consistent with the facts. The most satisfying interpretations of a selection are those that account for all the relevant facts. It is a good idea, therefore, to have your participants consider evidence that may contradict their opinions or require them to modify their positions. For example:

> *Leader:* Lynn, why does Jack succeed in this story?
>
> *Lynn:* It's all luck. Good things just happen to Jack.
>
> *Leader:* If it's all luck, why does the author refer to Jack as "sharp as a needle"?

There is no intent here to prove that the response is wrong. By inquiring into the validity of an answer, you are only helping the participant think about whether an idea is consistent with all the evidence in the text. In the above example, in response to the leader's follow-up question, Lynn might say, "The author is sarcastic in that statement. Jack isn't sharp, he's dumb. The author is making fun of Jack." Here, the leader's follow-up question has uncovered more fully the participant's point of view. By challenging interpretations, you help your participants develop the flexibility to expand upon or reconsider their initial assumptions and judgments.

   To select a line of inquiry. At any given moment in discussion, there are usually more good ideas expressed than you can work with at one time. Two participants may state opinions, one right after another, or one participant may offer a response with two good ideas in it, both worth pursuing. Decide which idea to pursue—keeping in mind both your basic question and your group's need for coherence in discussion—and then ask an appropriate follow-up question. To make sure you don't forget ideas that you may want to pursue later, jot them down on your seating chart. When you return to the idea, refer to the person who introduced it: "Amy said earlier...."

Transcript of a Sample Discussion: Asking Effective Follow-up Questions and Using a Prepared Cluster

The following transcript of segments of a discussion on "Jack and the Beanstalk" illustrates how you can use follow-up questions to manage the flow of ideas in discussion. Marginal notes identify the kinds of follow-up questions asked and indicate their function. In each instance, several different follow-up questions are possible. As you read through the transcript, think about how you would respond to what the participants say.

   The accompanying cluster will help you see what ideas the leader grappled with when preparing questions for discussion. You'll notice that at appropriate points in the discussion the leader makes use of a few of these cluster questions to follow up on participants' ideas. A prepared cluster can be an important resource if it is used properly. But leaders who rely too heavily on their cluster questions tend to ignore the responses of their participants. Prepared questions should never take the place of your on-the-spot follow-up questions, which reflect your reactions to what is being said. However, if you have prepared well, you will be able to trust your ability to recall the interpretive issues in the story, and you will usually end up using some of your cluster questions spontaneously, when they seem to fit naturally in the context of the discussion.

Basic Question: Why does Jack determine "to have another try at his luck" by climbing the beanstalk the third time?

Why isn't Jack "content" even though he has a limitless supply of gold from the magic hen?

Does Jack return a third time because he enjoys outsmarting the ogre?

Why isn't Jack afraid of being eaten by the ogre?

Why does Jack risk his life by taking the singing harp?

Soon after asking the basic question, the leader discovers that the group almost unanimously views Jack's primary motivation as greed and his risk-taking as selfish. Since the leader would not have asked the basic question if she had thought that it had only one reasonable answer, the challenge is to help make participants aware, through careful questioning, that the matter under discussion is probably more complex than the participants' immediate answers suggest.

Leader: [after asking the basic question and having the group write down answers] Alex, why does Jack determine "to have another try at his luck" by climbing the beanstalk the third time?

Alex: He got greedy.

Leader: What do you mean by "got greedy"?   Asks for clarification.

Alex: Well, he wasn't greedy the first two times. But by the third time he had the hen that would lay golden eggs. He wouldn't have to climb the stalk as long as the hen lived.

Leader: If he wasn't greedy at first, why do you think he became greedy?	Pursues an implication of Alex's response.
	As discussion continues, the leader finds that participants are unanimous so far in their response to the basic question, agreeing with Alex that Jack climbed the beanstalk a third time simply because he was greedy.

❖   ❖   ❖

Leader: Maria, do you also agree that Jack didn't become greedy until his third trip up the beanstalk?	Solicits an additional opinion. When the leader probes Maria's response, a different definition of greed emerges.
Maria: No. He was always greedy, like earlier when the cow went dry and he didn't want to have his mother worry about money anymore.	
Leader: Do you think Jack is being greedy when he wants to take care of his mother?	The leader pursues how Maria is defining greed.
Maria: Well, maybe it's not so much greedy as being afraid.	
Leader: Afraid of what?	Asks for clarification.
Maria: Afraid of what the future might hold?	
Leader: Then, Maria, does Jack climb the beanstalk for the third time because he is afraid of the future?	Returns to basic question, incorporating Maria's new insight; pursues an implication of her train of thought.
Maria: Maybe. Maybe he thought the hen would stop laying just like the cow went dry.	

Amy: I still think he was greedy from the very beginning. He sure wasn't thinking about anyone but himself when he made that stupid, selfish trade for the beans.

Leader: Amy, why do you think Jack was stupid to trade the dry cow for the magic beans?

> Asks for substantiation.

Amy: Well, Jack didn't know for sure that the beans were magic. He just made the trade without thinking about what his mother would say or what would happen next. Besides it's stupid to trust strange old men. In fact, I think the funny-looking man was working for the ogre. He had these beans that would make a stalk grow up to the ogre's house so he obviously went around giving them out so that the ogre would have plenty of little boys to eat.

Leader: Amy, can you show us evidence for your opinion that the old man works for the ogre?

> In order to prevent a possible digression (the old man is an agent of the ogre), the leader asks Amy to substantiate her opinion with evidence from the story.

Amy: Well, I guess I don't see any proof that the old man worked for the ogre, but I still don't think he's on Jack's side. On page 82, he says Jack is "sharp" but Jack really isn't at all. That proves the old man isn't honest.

Sam: I disagree. The old man means it when he says Jack is sharp. After all, Jack just gave a smart answer to that weird question "How many beans make five?" And besides, the old man told the truth: the beans really were magic and they helped Jack become rich.

Leader: So, Sam, was Jack being stupid and impulsive in trusting the old man or was he taking a pretty good risk?

The leader formulates a question combining Amy's and Sam's opposing points of view. In so doing, the leader makes it easier for the group to pursue the implications of Jack's risk-taking, ideas that are relevant to the basic question.

❖   ❖   ❖

Leader: Let's return now to our opening question and see what some other people have to say. Sarah, why do you think Jack went up the third time?

Asks the group to reconsider the basic question in light of the new thinking about Jack's character; solicits additional opinions.

Sarah: I think it was mostly out of greed. He realized it was easy to just go up and help himself to the giant's riches. But he also had a little bit of a sense of adventure. He wanted to outsmart the giant again...but the more I think about it, even that was selfish.

Tom: I think Jack is selfish, too, and always was. In the beginning of the story he doesn't have a job probably because he only thought about himself and was lazy.

Leader: Tom, if Jack was lazy, how do you account for the fact that we are told on the first page of the story that both Jack and his mother carried milk to the market every day?

Tests Tom's opinion that Jack was lazy by asking whether it is consistent with other evidence in the text. In challenging Tom's point, the leader opens the door to other interpretations of Jack.

Tom: I'll have to think about that.

Jeremy: Carrying milk every day seems like work to me. And just because Jack couldn't get a job doesn't mean he was lazy. He was probably too young. Besides, he's the one who volunteers to get work; his mother doesn't tell him to, she just wrings her hands and complains a lot.

Paula: He can't be lazy, Tom, because every time he goes up the beanstalk it says that he climbed and he climbed and he climbed and he climbed. A lazy person wouldn't have tried so hard.

Leader: That brings us back to what Sarah was saying earlier. Sarah, when you said it was "easy" for Jack to go up the third time, did you mean it wasn't dangerous...that Jack didn't need to be courageous and cunning?

Returns to Sarah's earlier comment to examine it in light of Paula's answer that Jack was not lazy. In asking Sarah to reconsider her thoughts about Jack, the leader pursues the line of inquiry opened up by Paula and Jeremy.

Sarah: No...I think he had to be smart to get away the third time....In fact, I think he got smarter each time he went to the giant's.

Leader: What in the story makes you think Jack gets smarter?

Asks for substantiation.

Sarah: It says on page 89 that "this time he knew better than to go straight to the ogre's house. And when he got near it he waited behind a bush till he saw the ogre's wife come out with a pail to get some water, and then he crept into the house and got into the copper."

Leader: How does that passage show that Jack is getting smarter?

Asks how the cited evidence supports Sarah's opinion.

Sarah: It shows he's planning. "He knew better than to go straight to the ogre's house." He figures the wife wouldn't be nice to him this time. And so he waits and hides until she comes out. Then he chooses a different hiding place, the copper instead of the oven.

Vanessa: I think he's getting smarter, too. And it seems like he's enjoying himself—fooling the giant and his wife, taking the harp right from under their noses—it's like a game for him.

Leader: Vanessa, how can something as scary as tricking a boy-eating ogre become a kind of game for Jack?

The leader chooses a line of inquiry, asking Vanessa to clarify her "game" interpretation, rather than to elaborate on her opinion that Jack is getting smarter. This leads to a consideration of Jack's sense of adventure.

Vanessa: Well, he has all the money he could possibly want from the hen and so, what's left for him to do except hang around the house with his mother? He can't do that forever. He needs to *do* something, take a few risks, or else he'll get bored. It was exciting the first two times up the beanstalk and so he went back to have an adventure.

Leader: Are you saying, Vanessa, that Jack takes this risky third trip because he is looking for kicks or because having adventures is a necessary part of growing up?

Pursues the implications in Vanessa's comments and moves the group toward the basic question.

❖   ❖   ❖

Leader: Colleen, why does the author have Jack take a singing harp on his third trip up the beanstalk?

Having explored the complexities of Jack's character, the group was ready to examine the meaning of Jack's third trip in the context of the story as a whole.

Colleen: I don't know.

Leader: Well, why does Jack risk his life by taking the singing harp?

Poses a prepared cluster question, and in so doing simplifies the question to ask Colleen to think about Jack's motivation rather than to consider the problem from the perspective of the author.

Colleen: I thought he took it because it was fun to take things that the giant really liked...and it seemed that the harp was extra special to the giant.

Leader: What makes you think the harp was extra special to the giant?

Asks for substantiation.

Colleen: Because it made beautiful music...it even sang him to sleep. When Jack took the harp, it called out to the giant, "Master! Master!"

Leader: Colleen, does taking a harp that makes beautiful music show that Jack is no longer satisfied with material comforts alone?

Incorporating one of Colleen's ideas, the leader returns to the problem of why Jack took the harp.

Colleen: I'm not sure....

Alex: Naah...Jack always took whatever the giant had out at the time. He would have taken anything.

Leader: But why does the author have Jack take on his third trip a singing harp—rather than some other kind of valuable object?

Reformulates the question to raise a possible intention of the author.

Colleen: To show that Jack didn't just want money...he
           wanted something that was beautiful *and*
           magical...having money wasn't enough to
           make Jack happy.

Alex: But it says at the end of the story that Jack
           showed the harp to get more money.

Colleen: [to Alex] But at least he's sharing it, not like
           the giant who kept it to himself. He's
           showing everyone that he conquered the
           giant and has his magic. And that's why Jack
           deserves to marry a princess.

Time was about to run
out, so the leader asked
participants if they each
had an answer to the
basic question they could
support with evidence
from the story, and to
consider how their initial
opinions had changed in
the course of discussion.
She also asked if anyone
had an answer that hadn't
been discussed.

This transcript illustrates how a leader uses follow-up questions, slowly and
persistently, to prompt the group to address and resolve the basic question.
Because of the leader's close interest and steady involvement, the participants
get caught up in striving for answers. They examine the text, begin to talk to one
another, build on their own ideas, and come to more comprehensive interpretations of the story.

RESOLUTION

Recognize when you reach a point of resolution; test it if necessary;
then either continue discussing the same basic question or begin
a new line of inquiry.

Resolution is that point in discussion when the group has heard and discussed a
number of answers to a basic question and when most participants could, if
asked, provide their own answers to the question and support them with evidence from the text. Resolution does not imply total agreement, or even a
majority opinion, about the answer to an interpretive question. Since basic
questions can have several satisfactory answers, it is likely that members of your

group will end up with different opinions. Nor is resolution a "wrapping up" of ideas; rather, it is a time for participants to recognize what interpretations have evolved as well as what might be discussed further.

One indication that your group has resolved a basic question is your own estimation that the interpretive issue in the question has been thoroughly examined and that further discussion is not likely to be productive. Other indications will come from your participants: they will begin to repeat themselves or to digress because they can say no more about the main question.

End before boredom sets in — or too much discussion

When you think your group has reached a point of resolution, repeat the basic question and call on members of the group to give the answers they remember hearing. Have your participants look back at their original written answers, and ask if anyone had an answer that was not discussed. This is also a good time to call on members of the group who did not participate very much ("Mick, did you hear an answer that made sense to you?"). After getting your participants to review the answers they remember, check your chart for any additional answers and ask participants about them: "Becky, didn't you have a different answer, something about...?" Or, "Liz, what was that other point you made about...?"

Encourage your participants to take a moment to compose their final answers to the basic question, taking into account the opinions and evidence offered by other members of the group. This synthesis is occurring naturally all through discussion, but now is the time to emphasize that even the most confidently held opinions can be improved by the ideas of others. Ask if anyone arrived at an answer that differs substantially from the one that he or she wrote down at the start of discussion. Then ask those participants who changed their minds to identify the ideas that seemed especially persuasive. Your participants will value shared inquiry more when they pause to consider how their own thinking has developed over the course of discussion.

In testing whether a basic question has been resolved, new ideas are often uncovered. In this way, your group will see that shared inquiry is a thinking process that does not necessarily end when discussion time is up. Post-discussion activities such as writing projects can encourage your participants to continue their interpretive work on a selection. But having successful discussions and demonstrating your own enthusiasm in the pursuit of ideas are the most effective ways to incite further reflection. ❖

3

Working with Your Participants in Shared Inquiry

OVERVIEW

This chapter explains how to introduce your participants to shared inquiry and how to help them develop their reading and discussion skills. If shared inquiry is a new experience for the members of your group, you will want to convey to them some of what you have learned in the Basic Leader Training Course. Like you, participants will need to know about the nature and aim of interpretive discussion, and about how to read actively, take notes, and write their own interpretive questions. This chapter also offers advice about how to cultivate among your participants an atmosphere of mutual respect, in which they feel free to share **their thoughts**, risk mistakes, and respond to and build upon the ideas of others. ❖

SUGGESTIONS FOR YOUR FIRST MEETING

For your Junior Great Books meetings, try to choose a room in which everyone can sit around a table; if this is not possible, have your participants sit in a circle or square. This type of arrangement stimulates discussion by making it possible for all members of the group to listen and talk directly to one another. It also helps reinforce the idea that your role in shared inquiry is that of a partner, and shows students that the ideas of their fellow participants will be a major source of help in gaining insight into a selection. Be sure your participants have a convenient surface where they can put their books down, open them up, and refer to them regularly. Discussion is very much an "open book" activity.

Begin your first meeting by explaining shared inquiry to your participants. Point out that the group will be reading and discussing a number of selections that have been chosen because they have literary merit and because their meaning is worth exploring. Emphasize that in shared inquiry leaders and participants learn from one another as they share questions and ideas about these readings. Explain that discussion will always center on a question that seems important to an understanding of the story or essay, and that you will not know the answer to the question.

Next, go over the four rules of discussion, explaining why the rules help participants think for themselves about the meaning of a selection (p. 22). Tell your participants that they are free to express any opinions or guesses that come to mind in response to your interpretive questions, even if they have not thought the ideas through. They need not wait to be called on; they may speak up at any time; and if they are called on but have nothing to say at the moment, they don't have to offer an answer.

Encourage your participants to listen to the ideas of their fellow students. Tell them that they can develop their own ideas by building on the thoughts of others, and that during discussion they can ask questions of others directly if there is something they do not understand.

If your group has not already read the first selection in the series you are using, have them read it at the first meeting. One of the reasons it has been placed first in the series is that it is short and can be read in twenty minutes or less. Even if participants have read the selection in advance, consider having them take turns reading it aloud at the first meeting. This can be especially helpful to those who are shy or less verbal because it gives them an easy way to begin speaking. Also, taking this step stresses the value of a second reading. Finally, hearing how participants read—or misread—the selection may give you ideas for new questions.

If participants are having difficulty with a word while reading aloud, it is best not to correct them. Instead, ask whether anybody in the group can help. Usually someone can, and after your first prompting or two, participants will begin to help one another spontaneously. For more on vocabulary in the Junior Great Books program, see page 57.

When you are ready to begin, follow the steps described in Chapter 2. Make up a seating chart and explain that it will help you keep track of—and draw connections between—the ideas that come up in discussion. Ask your basic question and have the students write it down. Then tell them to write down their answers; this gives them an opportunity to rally their initial ideas. At the end of discussion, find out if participants have reached a satisfying conclusion to your basic question (p. 39). Remind participants about the time of the next meeting and the selection they should read.

If at the end of discussion you feel there was not time to resolve certain questions or follow up on all the ideas—or perhaps correct what you think were certain misunderstandings on the part of your participants—don't be overly concerned. If the students have responded to your basic question, struggled with the text, begun to offer evidence for their opinions, and shown an interest in giving a fair hearing to the ideas of others—and especially if participants walk out the door still discussing the work among themselves—then you have made a fine start.

HELPING YOUR PARTICIPANTS
PREPARE FOR DISCUSSION

Participants should prepare for discussion in much the same way you do—by reading the selection twice and taking notes. Make sure they understand why it is important for them to do two separate readings. Explain that on a first reading they will probably concentrate on figuring out the plot; on a second reading, instead of wondering what will happen next, they can pay more attention to *why* things occur. They can see and reflect upon the story as a whole.

When introducing note-taking, encourage participants to mark anything that interests or puzzles them, anything they might want to remember for discussion. Use your own notes to demonstrate what you mean. After discussion, you may want to ask participants for examples of how their notes helped them remember an idea or piece of evidence, or how some of the passages or words they marked came up in discussion. In this way, you will make them aware that the parts of a story that intrigue individual readers, or give them pause, are often the very sections that require close interpretation and reward careful attention by the group.

The statements on method and the exercises that accompany the reading selections in Series Five and all later series will also help participants improve their preparation. For example, by studying the material on how to turn their notes into questions, participants learn to locate their own problems of interpretation before discussion and thus are able to bring more of their own ideas and concerns to the group. Here again, you can assist your participants by demonstrating how you write and refine your own interpretive questions.

GETTING YOUR PARTICIPANTS INVOLVED

For shared inquiry to work, your group members must feel that all their ideas and sudden insights—even their mistakes—are important steps in the process of building an interpretation. When participants feel confident that even their tentative opinions will be treated with respect, they are more inclined to risk expressing their thoughts.

One way to help your participants feel comfortable with sharing their ideas is to emphasize the creative nature of group inquiry. After discussion, call attention to the times when an opinion one participant was not sure of, and offered only tentatively, triggered an important insight in someone else. Illustrate how ideas are continually reevaluated by helping your group recall opinions that were abandoned and later, as a result of new insights, were found to have value. Remind participants that in discussion many ideas must be pooled before a satisfying interpretation can be realized, and that it's necessary to be open to change if the evidence demands it.

You may also want to ask your participants to assess informally how well they listened and responded to each other. Did they build interpretations as a group? Did they consider answers opposed to their own, and weigh the evidence in support of each possibility? Did they strive to pinpoint and resolve the story's important interpretive problems? You can use the comments on your seating chart or an audiotape of the discussion to help them in their assessment.

A good sign that participants are starting to feel at home with interpretive discussion is that they no longer respond exclusively to you; they talk directly to each other. Perhaps they will even anticipate some of your follow-up questions, by asking fellow participants for clarification or evidence. When participants see they can contribute to discussion not just by answering but by asking questions, they will become more attentive listeners. And active listening is as important to shared inquiry as active reading.

Finally, as you try to get your participants involved, remember that in shared inquiry you provide a model of a person who is curious about a problem and interested in pursuing a solution. Be patient and consistent and over time your participants will come to follow the habits of mind you display—of flexibility, open-mindedness, persistence, and curiosity. Demonstrating these habits throughout the program will have as much impact on your students as any individual discussion you might lead or particular skill you might teach.

HANDLING SOME COMMON DIFFICULTIES IN SHARED INQUIRY

Maintaining your role as leader is what sets the right atmosphere for your group to share ideas and think through problems. So when difficulties arise, as they do for even the most experienced leaders, continue to work within the framework of the rules of shared inquiry. Asking follow-up questions, just as you ordinarily do, should help you solve most types of problems.

One problem that leaders commonly encounter is digression. Because participants are encouraged to think freely, some of their comments may stray from the text and its meaning. When participants answer a question about a story by talking about their own feelings and experiences, ask a follow-up question to get them thinking again about the text:

> *Leader:* Allen, just before Scho falls, why does the author describe his voice as "exuberant and panicky"?
>
> *Allen:* I don't know. I know heights make *me* dizzy.
>
> *Leader:* Hmmm....why do you think being high in the tree makes Scho feel excited and afraid rather than dizzy?
>
> *Allen:* It can be scary, being up too high. Maybe he's afraid he's gone too far climbing, and with Monk and Glennie too.

Keep in mind that sometimes what seems like a digression may actually reflect a leap of mind into new territory. If you're not sure of the relevance of a response, ask the participant to furnish the connection. Getting participants to explain how their responses relate to the original question will prevent you from overlooking worthwhile ideas.

Sometimes a student will respond to your question by saying, "I don't know." This lack of response may simply mean that the participant didn't understand the question. Try rephrasing it:

Leader: Why does Scho enlarge the scope of his game
            at the end of the story?

Ann: I don't know.

Leader: At the end of the story, why does Scho say, "I
            want you to do whatever you're going to do
            for the whole rest of your life"?

Often, all the participant needs is additional time to let the question sink in. After a pause, if you continue to get no response, think of a passage that might clarify the problem and ask the participant to read it aloud. Then repeat your question. Try to stay with that person as long as you feel you are accomplishing something in striving for an answer. Then ask other participants to help out.

You can also use follow-up questions when participants forget important details or offer interpretations based on an incorrect reading of the story. To help your participants recall the facts, ask them to read and examine closely a relevant passage. This is also a good strategy when participants cannot locate the facts they need to support a reasonable opinion. Make sure your participants keep their books open throughout discussion. Encourage them to refer to the text often to look for examples and to check ideas.

If participants are having difficulty understanding a particular word or phrase in a story—and this becomes important in discussion—then use the word in a follow-up question meant to get students thinking about it. For instance, if students are not sure what the word "meek" means when applied to a character, ask them to describe that character and how he or she acts in different situations. Then ask, "Trish, is that what 'meek' means? Do you think a meek person acts in the way you've described?" This will give students a fuller concept of the word, and by asking them to paint a clearer picture of the character, you will be leading them more deeply into the story. If your group requires a more formal definition, ask someone to look the word up, but continue discussion until the dictionary definition can be introduced. Then ask participants to relate the dictionary meaning of the word to how it's used in the story. "Tom, can you think of times when Cinderella acts 'patient' and 'humble'?"

With experience, you will learn for yourself other problem-solving uses for follow-up questions. For instance, participants who dominate discussion can create problems by intimidating shy or less articulate participants into complete silence. You can check this in a positive, productive way by asking someone else to evaluate or comment upon one of the ideas offered by the overly talkative participant ("Sam, can you wait just a minute? Ann, do you agree with what Sam just said, that...?"). This strategy gets everyone's attention. It also selects a portion of the response to pursue, slows the rush of ideas, and involves other participants. An alternative is to ask talkative participants to respond to ideas they have not originated, thus encouraging them to listen more patiently to others in the group.

Participants who are initially rather shy and hesitant about expressing their ideas, or who tend merely to agree with their friends, can be drawn out if you show that their insights are useful to the group. Return to the ideas that they do express, and ask others in the group to consider them: "Bill, do you agree with Marcia's idea that...?" Be persistent in addressing questions to them by name and listening carefully to what they say.

There are also simple strategies for handling other kinds of problems that arise in discussion. If one or two students have not prepared, you might try asking them to sit outside the circle and read the story while discussion continues, and then rejoin the group. In some cases, there may be a general lack of interest in your basic question or all of your participants may seem stumped by it. Take some time to let the question take hold before deciding to drop it. Try rephrasing the question, or ask your participants to read aloud a passage or two that gave rise to the question and may help them see what the problem of meaning is. You might also want to check your cluster to look for an appropriate question that would help your participants begin to answer your basic question. If the group seems to be having trouble with the subject matter of the question, try to find out exactly what the difficulty is.

If your participants are resisting the selection as a whole, follow up specifically on why they didn't like it or couldn't get into it. Did they find it difficult to understand, perhaps because of unusual vocabulary or style? Did they find it boring or depressing? Did they dislike the way the characters act, or did certain incidents make them uncomfortable? Get your participants to point to passages that support their feelings, and ask them why the author included that information. What effect does it have on the rest of the story? Build on their dislike or lack of interest to get them into the selection. (You might also want to use textual analysis to help your group approach the selection. See the section that follows.) In handling this type of problem, keep in mind that liking a selection is not a prerequisite to having a good discussion. Interest in a work has a tendency to grow through shared inquiry; by working together, participants can often understand selections that put them off individually. They soon discover that they have more ideas to talk about than they initially realized.

Any discussion—with young people or adults—will have its share of wrong turns. Handle these as part of the normal process of shared inquiry, and your participants will learn to expect such difficulties from time to time and to feel confident that there are always ways to overcome them and get back into discussion. By dealing with problems within the context of your role as leader—as an asker of questions—you'll encourage the best creative and cooperative efforts of your group. Moreover, you'll minimize inhibitions caused by the fear of failure and help make discussion a freer, more comfortable exchange of ideas.

TEXTUAL ANALYSIS: HELPING YOUR GROUP EXAMINE A PASSAGE IN DETAIL

Textual analysis is a methodical way to look closely at a passage in a story or essay during discussion. In textual analysis, a group discusses a single passage line by line and sometimes word by word, raising questions about its meaning.

Something like textual analysis forms a regular part of discussion, when your question or a participant's evidence focuses the group's attention on a specific passage in the selection. The passage is read aloud, and the group reviews its context, examining specific words and phrases and seeing how they bear on the question under discussion. If participants cited the passage, encourage them to explain exactly how it backs up their ideas. Then ask others how the passage relates to their own opinions.

When participants are having an especially hard time with a text, a slower, more methodical approach to textual analysis can help them get a foothold. Ask them where their difficulty lies, or choose a passage yourself that seems important and challenging. Good possibilities are the opening or close of a selection, a crisis or a change of direction, or paragraphs that contain words and phrases the author seems to use in a special way.

First ask someone to read the passage aloud, while other members of the group follow in their books. This focuses attention and may give some participants the beginning of an understanding of what the passage means. Then ask questions to help the group review the context. In a story, ask who is speaking in the passage—author, fictional narrator, character—and recall what incidents have occurred up to that point. In nonfiction, ask about the position of the passage in the argument as a whole. If the passage is at the beginning, consider its purpose there. Does it introduce key terms or state the author's purpose? Does it describe a problem the author hopes to solve?

Next, go over the passage line by line, discussing any word, phrase, or sentence that puzzles or interests you or your participants. Essentially, you are brainstorming ideas about what the passage can mean. Untangle difficult sentences by asking about separate clauses and phrases. Work on difficult words by asking questions about their meaning in context and letting participants contribute their own or dictionary definitions. Invite your group to consider the author's specific choice of words; ask, "Why did the author select this particular way to say it?" Examine metaphors by asking about the comparisons they set up and their implications. While doing all this, try to remain open to all possibilities of meaning. Because every word in the story represents a decision the author has made, assume for the moment that everything might have importance in your understanding of the whole.

Encourage participants to contribute questions and to answer each other's questions if they can. Not all of their questions will be useful. Some may have factual answers that the group will readily supply. And others will have no answer at all in the text. In the process of asking questions, though, your group may uncover one or two new interpretive problems that can contribute significantly to discussion. Allow the group to discuss these briefly; and if they seem especially fruitful, write them down so you can go back to them after you have worked through the whole passage.

When the whole passage has been examined, ask participants if they can relate any new discoveries to what has already been discussed. Bring up again one of your prepared interpretive questions or return to one of the more interesting questions that your group raised during textual analysis.

The next page shows a leader's notes on a passage from "A Game of Catch," indicating the kinds of questions that could be raised in textual analysis. The leader has crossed out questions that lead nowhere and has marked with a star several questions that seem especially useful as springboards to discussion.

Does the title refer to Monk and Glennie's game of catch? Or also to Scho's game? How is Scho's game a "game of catch"?

A Game of Catch

Richard Wilbur

why does the author locate the game on the side lawn of The firehouse?

why does the author have Scho catch sight of Monk and Glennie before they see him?

why does the author give the boys such odd names?

what is meant by "good at it"?

Putting on a show?

MONK and Glennie were playing catch on the side lawn of the firehouse when Scho caught sight of them. They were good at it, for seventh-graders, as anyone could see right away. Monk, wearing a catcher's mitt, would lean easily sidewise and back, with one leg lifted and his throwing hand almost down to the grass, and then lob the white ball straight up into the sunlight. Glennie would shield his eyes with his left hand and, just as the ball fell past him, snag it with a little dart of his glove. Then he would burn the ball straight toward Monk, and it would spank into the round mitt and sit, like a still-life apple on a plate, until Monk flipped it over into his right hand and, with a negligent flick of his hanging arm, gave Glennie a fast grounder.

Does Scho see they are good at it?

why is it only Monk who has a specific kind of glove?

why does the author have them playing different positions?

why artistic terms to describe an athletic event?

unusual term, why negligent?

ADDITIONAL MATERIALS

Leader Aids are available for every series in the Junior Great Books program. These booklets review the main points covered in the Basic Leader Training Course in the context of the particular selections that you are using with your group. The Leader Aids contain essays on preparing for and leading discussion and offer advice on how to help your students prepare. They also include suggestions for helping students with unfamiliar vocabulary, preparing your group for more sophisticated selections, and using the stories in Junior Great Books as a basis for post-discussion writing assignments.

In addition to these essays, the Leader Aids also contain questions for each of the selections in a series. These questions are meant to stimulate your thinking about a selection; they are not intended as a substitute for your own efforts to generate interpretive questions. There may be times, however, when you have trouble writing enough questions to sustain discussion for a full period, or when your group becomes interested in an aspect of the selection for which you cannot formulate a question. If this should happen, our lists will help.

To help introduce students to shared inquiry, we have included in their books, beginning with Series Five, essays and exercises that cover such topics as the rules of discussion, active reading, taking notes, listening and responding to fellow participants, and writing interpretive questions. There are also occasional essays about aspects of stories such as character, theme, and setting, which will help students think interpretively about what they read. We recommend that before your first meeting you read through and become familiar with the exercises and statements in your participants' books as well as with the essays in your Leader Aid. ❖

4

About the Junior Great Books Program

CRITERIA FOR MAKING SELECTIONS

The stories and nonfiction selected for publication in the Junior Great Books series have passed through a stringent and lengthy review process. Selections are considered suitable for shared inquiry only if they meet the following four basic criteria:

> Selections must have a richness and complexity that will sustain an extended interpretive discussion.

> Selections must have literary merit and express meaningful ideas and themes, pertinent to the lives of children and adults alike.

> Selections must appeal to the age group reading a particular series.

> Selections must be limited in length so that participants can read a selection twice before their discussion group meets.

Our first criterion has to do with a selection's potential for interpretive discussion, and thus for fostering reflective reading and thinking in students. To determine whether a promising selection lends itself to interpretive discussion, each of two editors at the Foundation reads the selection several times and drafts a list of interpretive questions. The editors then meet to discuss their questions, offering as many answers to each question as come to mind and eliminating those questions that do not take them further into the text or illuminate its meaning.

Many selections are rejected as a result of this process. The text may simply be too slight to generate a multiplicity of questions and interpretations. Or the selection may be a very fine single-issue story, capable of being discussed, but for too limited a period of time. If the editors find themselves straining to come up with questions or answers, the story must be dropped.

On the other hand, the editors may write questions for a particular selection with great ease—only to discover in discussion that their questions cannot be fully answered by reference to the text alone. Or they may find that their questions, though satisfying the technical requirement of having two or more answers, fail to generate any real intellectual enthusiasm. And this is the ultimate test for a Junior Great Books selection. The editors involved in the evaluation process must feel that they have gained, through discussion, a fuller understanding of the story than they could have achieved on their own—that they have learned from each other.

If the selection is considered acceptable after this initial evaluation, it is then set aside until a third editor reviews the story and its accompanying interpretive questions—for we have found that some distance improves the accuracy of such a complicated series of judgments. The selection process culminates with a meeting in which all the editors involved decide on series placement and choose and refine the Leader Aid questions.

Our second criterion stresses that Junior selections must have as much meaning for adults as for children. This helps ensure that discussion will be a collaborative effort among leaders and students, with leaders' questions reflecting their genuine interest in a story. Selections that meet this double requirement, speaking both to children and to adults, are rare. Factors disqualifying a selection from consideration range from the obvious—explicit sexual references, for example—to the subtle: a story may be too elegiac or backward-looking for children to appreciate, or its tone may be too coolly analytical, too understated or restrained in sentiment.

Our third criterion emphasizes that a selection must appeal to the age group reading it. In the Junior program, the series number corresponds to grade level, with Series Five, for example, intended for the fifth grade. When deciding in which series a selection belongs, we place primary emphasis on appropriateness for the age group, rather than on standard assessments of reading levels for a particular grade.

For us, assessing whether a selection is suitable for a certain age group is often a matter of judging whether the philosophical or problematic ideas in a story are presented on a level that matches the child's intellectual and emotional growth. In the lower grades, for example, the folktales we publish are among the most popular—and the most readily discussible—selections in the entire Junior program. By presenting universal themes in a manner that can touch the inexperienced mind of the child, folktales give expression to many childhood concerns, such as the need for self-control as embodied in "The Fisherman and His Wife" and the struggle for independence as expressed in "Jack and the Beanstalk." Similarly, the modern children's stories in the lower series—such as those by Rumer Godden, Ted Hughes, and Philippa Pearce—treat themes that are particularly applicable to students in the primary grades.

In the middle grades, children's tastes begin to change. Although the magical and fantastic still has its appeal, students in these grades also wish to read stories that treat their concerns in more realistic contexts. This dictates a shift in the program toward including works by authors who write for an adult audience and yet vividly capture an experience of childhood in a manner that youngsters can understand and appreciate. By the time students reach high school, they are ready to read and discuss classic drama and short nonfiction selections from the traditional "great books." These types of selections are published, along with modern fiction, in Series Ten through Twelve.

But children's tastes are not our sole guide. Through continuing contact with group leaders nationwide, we maintain a good working knowledge of which stories are well received by most students and which have a narrower appeal. Although we would like to see every selection equally popular with all Junior Great Books participants, we are aware that some of the thought-provoking pieces that we publish may not immediately engage young readers. Nevertheless, it is our belief that most leaders, recognizing the merits of such selections, will meet this challenge and, through discussion, help their students overcome any initial difficulties, thus guiding them in broadening their tastes and ideas.

Our fourth criterion requires that our selections be limited in length. We keep selections as short as possible so that students will be better able to prepare thoroughly before a discussion. Response from the field has consistently called for shorter works. And our own experience confirms that the educational benefits children derive from reading a selection twice and reflecting on it before discussion are much greater than what they would gain by hurriedly reading a longer work, however fine.

This has been the rationale for providing only excerpts from some children's classics. Unfortunately, only a very few books lend themselves to this form of abridgment. For instance, our Series Seven selection from *Huckleberry Finn,* eleven consecutive chapters from the first half of the novel, is successful because the episodic nature of the story line provides a natural break. The same is true for *Dr. Dolittle* in Series Four. We found the excerpts from *The Wind in the Willows*—two chapters in Series Three and one in Four—to be reasonably self-contained since the questions they raise can be answered satisfactorily from the selections, without reference to the rest of the book.

The search for new selections is a slow and difficult one. Even with the abundance of new children's books published each year, it is not easy to find selections that suit our educative purposes. We keep a close watch on all new publications by screening national review periodicals, such as *Horn Book, Kirkus Reviews,* the *Bulletin of the Center for Children's Books,* and the American Library Association's *Booklist.* In addition, we subscribe to periodicals from England—where the tradition of children's literature is especially strong. We also look at the works in translation of recent outstanding children's writers, such as James Krüss and Tove Jansson, who are now represented in our second-semester series. And since much quality literature—especially children's—goes out of print very quickly, we spend a great deal of time combing libraries and used-book stores for anthologies and prize-winning books, works by particular authors, promising picture books, and possibly excerptable novels by relatively unrecognized writers.

Every seven or eight years, we revise the Junior Great Books series. The decision to drop some selections from our lists and add others is based mainly on information gathered from the field. We rely upon direct contact with teachers and administrators active in the program, as well as upon our staff's own experience in leading Junior groups. But, most importantly, we depend on the results of questionnaires that are distributed prior to any revision to thousands of active leaders nationwide.

In this questionnaire, leaders are asked to rate each selection they have used on the basis of student appeal, discussibility and grade-appropriateness. The leaders' answers help us determine not only which selections students enjoy reading initially, but also which stories "improve" after close analysis and discussion. Generally, we drop selections that do not have a high positive rating in these areas. At this writing, a majority of Junior selections have passed through one or more such evaluations.

The search for good selections is ongoing. We continue to consult reviews, periodicals, and educational journals, expanding our library with new children's books and significant works in the field of children's literature. It is vital for us to keep abreast of quality authors and to stay sensitive to the shifting trends and needs in our nation's schools, with the understanding that we can always improve the Junior Great Books series. In this effort, we invite your help.

VOCABULARY IN JUNIOR GREAT BOOKS

Each selection in Junior Great Books has been chosen for its richness for interpretive reading and discussion, and is published exactly as the author or translator wrote it. Because the vocabulary in selections is not simplified, and the range of vocabulary is exceptionally broad, students may need help in dealing with unfamiliar words, and with familiar words used in unfamiliar ways.

As you read a selection in preparation for discussion, you will begin to notice vocabulary that might be new to your participants. In looking over these words, try to distinguish between those that are significant for the meaning of the story or essay and those that seem less central to it. You may find yourself doing this naturally as you think about the interpretive problems that interest you. Some words, unusual or fairly ordinary, will give you pause, while others, though perhaps more exotic, will not raise your curiosity. We can explain this distinction more clearly by looking at some words in "Cinderella" (Series Two), which are almost certainly unfamiliar to students reading at grade level:

admirable	garret
aglow	haughtiest
brooch	liveried
cinders	parquet
coarse (applied to a person)	proper
coiffed	repulsive
curtsey	stays (in a woman's garment)
endured	unsurpassed
flattering	

Some of these words help create the setting or mood of the story, but do not figure in important interpretive issues in the work. Perhaps *coiffed, liveried, parquet,* and *stays* fit this description for you. Children will probably find, as you do, that these words are not essential to their growing understanding of the story, and will read right over them and figure out rough meanings from context. For example, reading that the stepsisters had "rooms with parquet floors," or that Cinderella, instead of leaving their hair "in a tangle," "coiffed them to perfection," children will gather that *parquet* is fancy flooring, and that *coiffed* is related to a nice hairdo.

Showing students how to search the context for clues to a word's meaning and asking them questions that guide them to do so are the best ways of encouraging this decoding of less significant vocabulary. Asking participants to memorize definitions for a long list of words chosen randomly from the story will only deflect them from their search for meaning in the story as a whole; besides, by removing the words from context, you remove the students' impetus for learning them. These "background" words, though never defined precisely and perhaps forgotten when the book is closed, serve their purpose by conveying to young readers a sense of style.

But there is another category of unfamiliar words—those that seem directly related to problems of meaning—that will be in the "foreground" of your thinking about a story. It is easy to see how readers of "Cinderella" might want to consider the meanings of *cinders, haughtiest,* or *unsurpassed* as they answer an interpretive question such as "Why is Cinderella kind to the stepmother and stepsisters who mistreat her?" In your preparation, you will have found the words that seem to you especially intriguing and important. In addition, your students' own ideas about the story might lead them to ask about or comment on words that had not caught your attention but that seem to deserve the group's careful thought. Words that appear to you or your participants as key terms in the story should be explored during the course of discussion.

To do this effectively, deal with a difficult word as you would any point needing clarification. First ask for a rough definition—the participants' own or the dictionary's. (The rules of discussion do not permit you to offer one.) Then, in follow-up questions, inquire about the word's connotations in context, and the author's possible reasons for using that particular word rather than another. Guide participants to relate what is said about the word to the interpretive question being discussed. In this way, they will see how the meaning of a word both derives from and contributes to the context in which it is used.

Even seemingly commonplace words, such as the word *beautiful* in "Cinderella," may carry a great weight of meaning within a given work. This is especially true of Junior Great Books selections for high school students. For instance, in Immanuel Kant's "Conscience" (Series Twelve), *conscience, judgment,* and *instinct* might seem well known, but have meanings that are elusive in the way Kant uses them. "The Declaration of Independence" (Series Eleven) abounds with long words such as *annihilation, consanguinity,* and *usurpation;* but discussion might center more fruitfully on interpreting the full significance of the seemingly simple *one people,* or *right.* As your students come to see that an interpretation can turn on the possible meanings of a single word, their interest in exploring unfamiliar vocabulary will grow. In time, handling new words will become a natural and regular part of their effort to understand what they read.

CURRICULUM OBJECTIVES

The objectives of the Junior Great Books program include strengthening reading comprehension and promoting higher-level thinking, as well as developing oral language skills. You may want to consider these components of the program as you plan lessons and work with students. But keep in mind that we have set the skills out separately here for analytical purposes only. In shared inquiry, students will use a combination of all these skills to further their understanding and enjoyment of what they read.

Listening

In discussion, participants listen and respond to the leader's questions, as well as to the statements of fellow participants. The leader models listening skills by paying close attention to participants' comments, taking notes on them, and posing questions that directly respond to them. The leader also encourages active listening and a cooperative attitude by asking questions that get participants to respond to each other's statements and to assist one another in recalling facts and explaining opinions.

Speaking

Shared inquiry discussion requires that participants present opinions, explain reasons for an inference or conclusion, use persuasion, recite facts, recount others' opinions, and read aloud. The leader helps students achieve more coherent, varied, and complex oral expression by slowing the pace of discussion, encouraging participants to speak directly to each other, and asking thoughtful follow-up questions. In addition, by showing respect for participants and interest in their ideas, the leader helps them learn to offer differing opinions firmly but politely, and to maintain an orderly discussion.

Reading

Reading skills are exercised at every stage in the process of shared inquiry. Students develop their comprehension by such activities as reading a story carefully twice, taking notes, doing preparatory work with unfamiliar vocabulary, writing original interpretive questions, and carrying out textual analysis.

Deriving word meanings from context. This occurs as students explain the meaning of those passages they cite as evidence, and, in many cases, as they answer the leader's interpretive question.

Recalling details. In citing evidence from the selection for an answer to an interpretive question, participants recall details and often organize details as well.

Organizing details (time sequence, cause and effect). Students mentally arrange details in logical orders as they master the facts of the selection and weigh and compare evidence cited to support different opinions. The leader prompts students to organize details and to explain how they have done so by asking for support for their positions and for clarification.

Drawing inferences. Answering both interpretive and factual questions involves drawing inferences from the details in the selection. Follow-up questions asking students to clarify ideas often lead them to explain the inferences they have drawn.

Recognizing tone and point of view. Students' and leaders' interpretive "author" questions frequently focus on the tone and point of view of passages or a whole selection. Follow-up questions asking students how they read specific passages or how they reconcile seemingly contradictory facts in the text usually require them to consider the author's stance towards characters and events as well as the perspective from which the story is told.

Understanding characters. The motivation of characters is probably the most common source of students' and leaders' interpretive questions about stories; discussions frequently center on why characters in stories act as they do.

Finding the main idea of a paragraph. In writing interpretive questions, students find the main idea not only in one paragraph but in several paragraphs, and sometimes juxtapose two different central ideas to present a problem of meaning in the selection. In discussion, the leader gets students to find the main idea and to explain how they found it through close textual analysis and follow-up questions that ask students to summarize passages cited as evidence.

Drawing conclusions; finding the main idea of the text as a whole. Answering basic questions in discussion involves finding and weighing possible "main ideas" for the whole selection. Students also explore comprehensive interpretive issues and major themes when they write their own questions. In resolution, students sum up their own conclusions about the meaning of the work and consider other possible conclusions.

Thinking

Consecutive, reflective thinking is called upon in shared inquiry as students explain their opinions and the evidence supporting them, comment on others' statements, try to use evidence brought up by others, and modify their own thinking to make use of the ideas they hear.

Problem-solving. Answering a leader's interpretive question, orally or in writing, involves recognizing the problem that it poses and generating an original idea to resolve that problem.

Argument. In supporting an answer to an interpretive question, a student clarifies the opinion, explains the reasons behind it, and offers logical support in the form of evidence from the selection. Usually, the participant must respond to points of view already stated and evidence already brought forward by classmates.

Critical thinking, analysis. To give an opinion on statements made by classmates, a student must analyze the arguments, assessing their logic and the evidence offered to support them.

Synthesis. Answering a basic question during discussion involves bringing together many facts from the story and ideas about them into a single coherent statement. In resolution, students elaborate on their own initial opinions, accommodating ideas and evidence cited by other participants and reconciling or choosing among conflicting lines of thought.

PROGRAM ORGANIZATION

Nationwide, there is great variation in the way Junior Great Books programs are organized and administered. In each case, trained leaders get together with a number of participants to interpret reading selections provided by the Foundation. These three elements—trained leaders, participants, and specially selected works—are virtually the only constants in the way programs are organized. Still, by monitoring the various ways our program has been used over the years and is being used today, we can describe what is typical and preferable in most programs.

Scheduling

Almost all Junior Great Books groups meet during the regular school day at least once a week; individual discussions last as long as the usual time periods for each grade level. The scheduled time is often a regular class period, the library hour, or a study period. Whatever time is selected, administrators and leaders agree that it is best if the group meets at the same time each week. When Great Books is part of the school reading program, two periods are often scheduled: the first to ensure that students have time to read the selection twice, and the second for discussion. Occasionally, a third hour is scheduled for post-discussion activities.

Each Junior program runs twelve weeks to correspond to the twelve reading selections in a series. Second-semester series are available for grades three, four, five, and six. These series are intended for groups that have completed one semester of Junior Great Books and require additional reading selections for the second part of the school year.

Who Participates

The current Junior Great Books program is designed for students from the second through the twelfth grade. In the near future, we plan to add a read-aloud program for younger children. Because good reading and thinking habits take time to develop, it is best if students begin Great Books early and have an opportunity to participate year after year in an unbroken sequence.

Some schools and school districts select certain students for Great Books groups in order to achieve particular educational objectives. Gifted children might be pulled out of regular classes to participate. Conversely, students who are not doing as well as they should are sometimes assigned to a Great Books group as a way of helping them bring their skills up to par. Because disciplined discussion encourages interest in reading and stretches participants' ability to think about what they have read, students at all levels seem to benefit from participation in the program.

Group Size

Fifteen to twenty students make up a good-sized group, but many school districts use their normal classes for the program—as many as thirty or thirty-five students. While participants benefit from the more varied input that is possible in larger groups, they also profit from the greater attention they receive in smaller groups. There are obvious disadvantages to extremes in either direction—from a group so small that it has difficulty sustaining an extended discussion, to one so large that some participants don't get a chance to speak. But many programs operate successfully with groups that would seem too large or too small to other districts.

Selecting the Appropriate Series of Readings

The number of each series corresponds to recommended grade level, and most programs find this appropriate. To assist less able readers, it is occasionally advisable to use an earlier series of selections, though experience shows that students will not be receptive to selections that are more than one grade level below their own. On the other hand, there is no evidence supporting the use of a higher series for better readers: leaders find that the selections are sufficiently rich to challenge even the best readers at each level. ❖

—APPENDIX—

MATERIALS
—for the—
BASIC LEADER
TRAINING COURSE

SCHOOL OF EDUCATION
CURRICULUM LABORATORY
UM-DEARBORN

Q1 Why is Jack rewarded rather than punished for stealing from the ogre?
   (time to think of answer, jot notes, evidence)
   - ogre was bad; eating other little boys

Was Jack smart?
Was the mother responsible?
Why does Jack think the trade would be good?

   Cunning — survival technique

Follow up questions
- ask for clarification — don't clarify for them
- ask for proof, evidence
- develop idea
- ask for evaluation

Jack and the Beanstalk

Told by Joseph Jacobs

THERE was once upon a time a poor widow who had an only son named Jack and a cow named Milky-white. And all they had to live on was the milk the cow gave every morning, which they carried to the market and sold. But one morning Milky-white gave no milk and they didn't know what to do.

"What shall we do, what shall we do?" said the widow, wringing her hands.

"Cheer up, mother, I'll go and get work somewhere," said Jack.

"We've tried that before, and nobody would take you," said his mother. "We must sell Milky-white and with the money start a shop or something."

"All right, mother," says Jack. "It's market day today, and I'll soon sell Milky-white, and then we'll see what we can do."

So he took the cow's halter in his hand, and off he started. He hadn't gone far when he met a funny-looking old man who said to him: "Good morning, Jack."

"Good morning to you," said Jack, and wondered how he knew his name.

"Well, Jack, and where are you off to?" said the man.

"I'm going to market to sell our cow here."

"Oh, you look the proper sort of chap to sell cows," said the man. "I wonder if you know how many beans make five."

riddle?? .

"Two in each hand and one in your mouth," says Jack, as sharp as a needle.

"Right you are," says the man. "And here they are, the very beans themselves," he went on, pulling out of his pocket a number of strange-looking beans. "As you are so sharp," says he, "I don't mind doing a swap with you—your cow for these beans."

"Go along," says Jack. "Wouldn't you like it?"

"Ah! you don't know what these beans are," said the man. "If you plant them overnight, by morning they grow right up to the sky."

"Really?" says Jack. "You don't say so."

"Yes, that is so, and if it doesn't turn out to be true you can have your cow back."

"Right," says Jack, and hands him over Milky-white's halter and pockets the beans.

Back goes Jack home, and as he hadn't gone very far it wasn't dusk by the time he got to his door.

"Back already, Jack?" said his mother. "I see you haven't got Milky-white, so you've sold her. How much did you get for her?"

"You'll never guess, mother," says Jack.

"No, you don't say so. Good boy! Five pounds, ten, fifteen, no, it can't be twenty."

"I told you you couldn't guess. What do you say to these beans; they're magical, plant them overnight and—"

abuse?.

"What!" says Jack's mother. "Have you been such a fool, such a dolt, such an idiot, as to give away my Milky-white, the best milker in the parish, and prime beef to boot, for a set of paltry beans? Take that! Take that! Take that! And as for your precious beans, here they go out of the window. And now off with you to bed. Not a sip shall you drink, and not a bit shall you swallow this very night."

So Jack went upstairs to his little room in the attic, and sad and sorry he was, to be sure, as much for his mother's sake as for the loss of his supper.

At last he dropped off to sleep.

When he woke up, the room looked so funny. The sun was shining into part of it, and yet all the rest was quite dark and shady. So Jack jumped up and dressed himself and went to the window. And what do you think he saw? Why, the beans his mother had thrown out of the window into the garden had sprung up into a big beanstalk which went up and up and up till it reached the sky. So the man spoke truth after all.

The beanstalk grew up quite close past Jack's window, so all he had to do was to open it and give a jump onto the beanstalk, which ran up just like a big ladder. So Jack climbed, and he climbed and he climbed and he climbed and he climbed and he climbed and he climbed till at last he reached the sky. And when he got there he found a long broad road going as straight as a dart. So he walked along and he walked along and he walked along till he came to a great big tall house, and on the doorstep there was a great big tall woman.

"Good morning, mum," says Jack, quite polite-like. "Could you be so kind as to give me some breakfast?" For he hadn't had anything to eat, you know, the night before and was as hungry as a hunter.

"It's breakfast you want, is it?" says the great big tall woman. "It's breakfast you'll be if you don't move off from here. My man is an ogre and there's nothing he likes better than boys broiled on toast. You'd better be moving on or he'll soon be coming."

"Oh! please mum, do give me something to eat, mum. I've had nothing to eat since yesterday morning, really and truly, mum," says Jack. "I may as well be broiled as die of hunger."

Well, the ogre's wife was not half so bad after all. So she took Jack into the kitchen and gave him a chunk of bread and cheese and a jug of milk. But Jack hadn't half finished these when thump! thump! thump! the whole house began to tremble with the noise of someone coming.

"Goodness gracious me! It's my old man," said the ogre's wife. "What on earth shall I do? Come along quick and jump in here." And she bundled Jack into the oven just as the ogre came in.

He was a big one, to be sure. At his belt he had three calves strung up by the heels, and he unhooked them and threw them down on the table and said: "Here, wife, broil me a couple of these for breakfast. Ah! what's this I smell?

Fee-fi-fo-fum,

I smell the blood of an Englishman,

Be he alive, or be he dead

I'll grind his bones to make my bread."

"Nonsense, dear," said his wife, "you're dreaming. Or perhaps you smell the scraps of that little boy you liked so much for yesterday's dinner. Here, you go and have a wash and tidy up, and by the time you come back your breakfast will be ready for you."

So off the ogre went, and Jack was just going to jump out of the oven and run away when the woman told him not. "Wait till he's asleep," says she. "He always has a doze after breakfast."

Well, the ogre had his breakfast, and after that he goes to a big chest and takes out a couple of bags of gold, and down he sits and counts till at last his head began to nod and he began to snore till the whole house shook again.

Then Jack crept out on tiptoe from his oven, and as he was passing the ogre he took one of the bags of gold under his arm, and off he pelters till he came to the beanstalk, and then he threw down the bag of gold, which of course fell into his mother's garden, and then he climbed down and climbed down till at last he got home and told his mother and showed her the gold and said: "Well, mother, wasn't I right about the beans. They are really magical, you see."

So they lived on the bag of gold for some time, but at

& greedy

last they came to the end of it, and Jack made up his mind
to try his luck once more up at the top of the beanstalk. So
one fine morning he rose up early and got onto the beanstalk, and he climbed and he climbed and he climbed
and he climbed and he climbed and he climbed till at last he
came out onto the road again and up to the great big tall
house he had been to before. There, sure enough, was the
great big tall woman standing on the doorstep.

"Good morning, mum," says Jack, as bold as brass.
"Could you be so good as to give me something to eat?"

"Go away, my boy," said the big tall woman, "or else my
man will eat you up for breakfast. But aren't you the
youngster who came here once before? Do you know, that
very day, my man missed one of his bags of gold."

"That's strange, mum," says Jack. "I dare say I could tell
you something about that, but I'm so hungry I can't speak
till I've had something to eat."

Well the big tall woman was so curious that she took
him in and gave him something to eat. But he had scarcely
begun munching it as slowly as he could when thump!
thump! thump! they heard the giant's footstep, and his
wife hid Jack away in the oven.

All happened as it did before. In came the ogre as he did
before, said "Fee-fi-fo-fum," and had his breakfast of three
broiled oxen. Then he said: "Wife, bring me the hen that
lays the golden eggs." So she brought it, and the ogre said
"Lay," and it laid an egg all of gold. And then the ogre
began to nod his head and to snore till the house shook.

Then Jack crept out of the oven on tiptoe and caught
hold of the golden hen, and was off before you could say
"Jack Robinson." But this time the hen gave a cackle which
woke the ogre, and just as Jack got out of the house he
heard him calling: "Wife, wife, what have you done with
my golden hen?"

And the wife said: "Why, my dear?"

But that was all Jack heard, for he rushed off to the beanstalk and climbed down like a house on fire. And when he got home he showed his mother the wonderful hen and said "Lay," to it; and it laid a golden egg every time he said "Lay."

 Well, Jack was not content, and it wasn't very long before he determined to have another try at his luck up there at the top of the beanstalk. So one fine morning he rose up early, and got onto the beanstalk, and he climbed and he climbed and he climbed and he climbed till he got to the top. But this time he knew better than to go straight to the ogre's house. And when he got near it he waited behind a bush till he saw the ogre's wife come out with a pail to get some water, and then he crept into the house and got into the copper. He hadn't been there long when he heard thump! thump! thump! as before, and in come the ogre and his wife.

"Fee-fi-fo-fum, I smell the blood of an Englishman," cried out the ogre. "I smell him, wife, I smell him."

"Do you, my dearie?" says the ogre's wife. "Then if it's that little rogue that stole your gold and the hen that laid the golden eggs, he's sure to have got into the oven." And they both rushed to the oven. But Jack wasn't there, luckily, and the ogre's wife said: "There you are again with your fee-fi-fo-fum. Why of course it's the boy you caught last night that I've just broiled for your breakfast. How forgetful I am, and how careless you are not to know the difference between live and dead after all these years."

So the ogre sat down to the breakfast and ate it, but every now and then he would mutter: "Well, I could have sworn—" and he'd get up and search the larder and the cupboards, and everything, only luckily he didn't think of the copper.

After breakfast was over, the ogre called out: "Wife, wife, bring me my golden harp." So she brought it and put it on the table before him. Then he said "Sing!" and the golden harp sang most beautifully. And it went on singing till the ogre fell asleep and commenced to snore like thunder.

Then Jack lifted up the copper lid very quietly and got down like a mouse and crept on hands and knees till he came to the table, when up he crawled, caught hold of the golden harp, and dashed with it towards the door. But the harp called out quite loud "Master! Master!" and the ogre woke up just in time to see Jack running off with his harp.

Jack ran as fast as he could, and the ogre came rushing after, and would soon have caught him only Jack had a start and dodged him a bit and knew where he was going. When he got to the beanstalk the ogre was not more than twenty yards away, when suddenly he saw Jack disappear, and when he came to the end of the road he saw Jack underneath climbing down for dear life. Well, the ogre didn't like trusting himself to such a ladder, and he stood and waited, so Jack got another start. But just then the harp cried out "Master! Master!" and the ogre swung himself down onto the beanstalk, which shook with his weight.

Down climbs Jack, and after him climbed the ogre. By this time Jack had climbed down and climbed down and climbed down till he was very nearly home. So he called out: "Mother! Mother! Bring me an axe, bring me an axe." And his mother came rushing out with the axe in her hand, but when she came to the beanstalk she stood stock-still with fright for there she saw the ogre with his legs just through the clouds.

But Jack jumped down and got hold of the axe and gave a chop at the beanstalk which cut it half in two. The ogre felt the beanstalk shake and quiver so he stopped to see what was the matter. Then Jack gave another chop with the axe, and the beanstalk was cut in two and began to topple over. Then the ogre fell down and broke his crown, and the beanstalk came toppling after.

Jack and Jill

money solves everything!!..

Then Jack showed his mother his golden harp, and what with showing that and selling the golden eggs, Jack and his mother became very rich, and he married a great princess, and they lived happy ever after. ❖

PREPARE STORY

- read twice, become familiar
  see diff. or more details in second reading
- take notes, actively read, react to text
  same guidelines as p.67   start simple with younger
  easier to find evidence   kids or new stories
* ie. "put ? on things you don't understand"
  "put ! on things that surprise you"

A Game of Catch

[handwritten: Who gets caught in the game of catch?]

[handwritten: Series 6]

Richard Wilbur

[handwritten: — puzzle, — reaction, strongly to, — important to story]

MONK and Glennie were playing catch on the side lawn of the firehouse when Scho caught sight of them. They were good at it, for seventh-graders, as anyone could see right away. Monk, wearing a catcher's mitt, would lean easily sidewise and back, with one leg lifted and his throwing hand almost down to the grass, and then lob the white ball straight up into the sunlight. Glennie would shield his eyes with his left hand and, just as the ball fell past him, snag it with a little dart of his glove. Then he would burn the ball straight toward Monk, and it would spank into the round mitt and sit, like a still-life apple on a plate, until Monk flipped it over into his right hand and, with a negligent flick of his hanging arm, gave Glennie a fast grounder.

[handwritten: why is it significant to be seventh-graders]

They were going on and on like that, in a kind of slow, mannered, luxurious dance in the sun, their faces perfectly blank and entranced, when Glennie noticed Scho dawdling along the other side of the street and called hello to him. Scho crossed over and stood at the front edge of the lawn, near an apple tree, watching.

[handwritten: metaphor]

"Got your glove?" asked Glennie after a time. Scho obviously hadn't.

[handwritten: asked even though he knew he couldn't play]

"You could give me some easy grounders," said Scho. "But don't burn 'em."

75

"All right," Glennie said. He moved off a little, so the three of them formed a triangle, and they passed the ball around for about five minutes, Monk tossing easy grounders to Scho, Scho throwing to Glennie, and Glennie burning them in to Monk. After a while, Monk began to throw them back to Glennie once or twice before he let Scho have his grounder, and finally Monk gave Scho a fast, bumpy grounder that hopped over his shoulder and went into the brake on the other side of the street.

didn't play fair

"Not so hard," called Scho as he ran across to get it.

"You should've had it," Monk shouted.

It took Scho a little while to find the ball among the ferns and dead leaves, and when he saw it, he grabbed it up and threw it toward Glennie. It struck the trunk of the apple tree, bounced back at an angle, and rolled steadily and stupidly onto the cement apron in front of the firehouse, where one of the trucks was parked. Scho ran hard and stopped it just before it rolled under the truck, and this time he carried it back to his former position on the lawn and threw it carefully to Glennie.

not a good ball

plot?

"I got an idea," said Glennie. "Why don't Monk and I catch for five minutes more, and then you can borrow one of our gloves?"

2 · not fair

"That's all right with me," said Monk. He socked his fist into his mitt, and Glennie burned one in.

"All right," Scho said, and went over and sat under the tree. There in the shade he watched them resume their skillful play. They threw lazily fast or lazily slow—high, low, or wide—and always handsomely, their expressions serene, changeless, and forgetful. When Monk missed a low backhand catch, he walked indolently after the ball and, hardly even looking, flung it sidearm for an imaginary put-out. After a good while of this, Scho said, "Isn't it five minutes yet?"

"One minute to go," said Monk, with a fraction of a grin.

plot

What were Scho's intentions in climbing the tree?

Did Scho want to play ball?

Scho stood up and watched the ball slap back and forth for several minutes more, and then he turned and pulled himself up into the crotch of the tree.

"Where are you going?" Monk asked.

"Just up the tree," Scho said.

"I guess he doesn't want to catch," said Monk.

Scho starts own plot

Scho went up and up through the fat light-gray branches until they grew slender and bright and gave under him. He found a place where several supple branches were knit to make a dangerous chair, and sat there with his head coming out of the leaves into the sunlight. He could see the two other boys down below, the ball going back and forth between them as if they were bowling on the grass, and Glennie's crew-cut head looking like a sea urchin.

Why did he choose such a dangerous spot?

suggestive

"I found a wonderful seat up here," Scho said loudly. "If I don't fall out." Monk and Glennie didn't look up or comment and so he began jouncing gently in his chair of branches and singing "Yo-ho, heave ho" in an exaggerated way.

cause/effect Was he looking for attention?

"Do you know what, Monk?" he announced in a few moments. "I can make you two guys do anything I want. Catch that ball, Monk! Now you catch it, Glennie!"

"I was going to catch it anyway," Monk suddenly said. "You're not making anybody do anything when they're already going to do it anyway."

why was he aggrevating the boys?

"I made you say what you just said," Scho replied joyfully.

"No, you didn't," said Monk, still throwing and catching but now less serenely absorbed in the game.

cause/effect

"That's what I wanted you to say," Scho said.

The ball bounded off the rim of Monk's mitt and plowed into a gladiolus bed beside the firehouse, and Monk ran to get it while Scho jounced in his treetop and sang, "I wanted you to miss that. Anything you do is what I wanted you to do."

"Let's quit for a minute," Glennie suggested.

Didn't want to give him attention

"We might as well, until the peanut gallery shuts up," Monk said.

trying not to take him seriously

THEY went over and sat crosslegged in the shade of the tree. Scho looked down between his legs and saw them on the dim, spotty ground, saying nothing to one another. Glennie soon began abstractedly spinning his glove between his palms; Monk pulled his nose and stared out across the lawn.

"I want you to mess around with your nose, Monk," said Scho, giggling. Monk withdrew his hand from his face.

"Do that with your glove, Glennie," Scho persisted. "Monk, I want you to pull up hunks of grass and chew on it."

Glennie looked up and saw a self-delighted, intense face staring down at him through the leaves. "Stop being a dope and come down and we'll catch for a few minutes," he said.

only impressing himself?

Scho hesitated, and then said, in a tentatively mocking voice, "That's what I wanted you to say."

Is Scho still confident of his game?

"All right, then, nuts to you," said Glennie.

"Why don't you keep quiet and stop bothering people?" Monk asked.

"I made you say that," Scho replied, softly.

"Shut up," Monk said.

why do Glen and Monk fall for his game?

"I made you say that, and I want you to be standing there looking sore. And I want you to climb up the tree. I'm making you do it!"

Monk was scrambling up through the branches, awkward in his haste, and getting snagged on twigs. His face was furious and foolish, and he kept telling Scho to shut up, shut up, shut up, while the other's exuberant and panicky voice poured down upon his head.

"Now you shut up or you'll be sorry," Monk said,

breathing hard as he reached up and threatened to shake the cradle of slight branches in which Scho was sitting.

"I *want*—" Scho screamed as he fell. Two lower branches broke his rustling, crackling fall, but he landed on his back with a deep thud and lay still, with a strangled look on his face and his eyes clenched. Glennie knelt down and asked breathlessly, "Are you O.K., Scho? Are you O.K.?" while Monk swung down through the leaves crying that honestly he hadn't even touched him, the crazy guy just let go. Scho doubled up and turned over on his right side, and now both the other boys knelt beside him, pawing at his shoulder and begging to know how he was.

Then Scho rolled away from them and sat partly up, still struggling to get his wind but forcing a species of smile into his face.

"I'm sorry, Scho," Monk said. "I didn't mean to make you fall."

Scho's voice came out weak and gravelly, in gasps. "I meant—you to do it. You—had to. You can't do— anything—unless I want—you to."

Glennie and Monk looked helplessly at him as he sat there, breathing a bit more easily and smiling fixedly, with tears in his eyes. Then they picked up their gloves and the ball, walked over to the street, and went slowly away down the sidewalk, Monk punching his fist into the mitt, Glennie juggling the ball between glove and hand.

From under the apple tree, Scho, still bent over a little for lack of breath, croaked after them in triumph and misery, "I want you to do whatever you're going to do for the whole rest of your life!" ❖

[handwritten marginalia:]
Did Scho fall on his own?
what is Scho's game?
Was Scho really in control up in the tree?
Who triumphed?
How did Scho triumph yet still feel miserable?

THUCYDIDES' History of the Peloponnesian War *describes the conflict between Athens and Sparta that took place between 431 and 404* B.C. *and involved most of the Greek city-states on one side or the other. Melos, a small island off the southeastern coast of Greece, tried to remain independent and neutral, resisting an Athenian attempt to make it a tributary. Athens then sent a second expedition to subjugate the island, or at least to force it into an alliance. Before giving the order to attack, the Athenian generals sent representatives to negotiate with the Melians.*

The Melian Dialogue

Thucydides

THE NEXT SUMMER the Athenians made an expedition against the island of Melos. The Melians are a colony of Lacedaemon that would not submit to the Athenians like the other islanders and at first remained neutral and took no part in the struggle, but afterwards, upon the Athenians using violence and plundering their territory, assumed an attitude of open hostility. The Athenian generals encamped in their territory with their army, and before doing any harm to their land sent envoys to negotiate. These the Melians did not bring before the people, but told them to state the object of their mission to the magistrates and the council. The Athenian envoys then said:

ATHENIANS: As we are not to speak to the people, for fear that if we made a single speech without interruption we might deceive them with attractive arguments to which there was no chance of replying — we realize that this is the meaning of our being brought before your ruling body — we suggest that you who sit here should make security doubly sure. Let us have no long speeches from you either, but deal separately with each point, and take up at once any statement of which you disapprove, and criticize it.

A selection from *The History of the Peloponnesian War.*

81

MELIANS: We have no objection to your reasonable suggestion that we should put our respective points of view quietly to each other, but the military preparations which you have already made seem inconsistent with it. We see that you have come to be yourselves the judges of the debate, and that its natural conclusion for us will be slavery if you convince us, and war if we get the better of the argument and therefore refuse to submit.

ATHENIANS: If you have met us in order to make surmises about the future, or for any other purpose than to look existing facts in the face and to discuss the safety of your city on this basis, we will break off the conversations; otherwise, we are ready to speak.

MELIANS: In our position it is natural and excusable to explore many ideas and arguments. But the problem that has brought us here is our security, so, if you think fit, let the discussion follow the line you propose.

ATHENIANS: Then we will not make a long and unconvincing speech, full of fine phrases, to prove that our victory over Persia justifies our empire, or that we are now attacking you because you have wronged us, and we ask you not to expect to convince us by saying that you have not injured us, or that, though a colony of Lacedaemon, you did not join her. Let each of us say what we really think and reach a practical agreement. You know and we know, as practical men, that the question of justice arises only between parties equal in strength, and that the strong do what they can, and the weak submit.

MELIANS: As you ignore justice and have made self-interest the basis of discussion, we must take the same ground, and we say that in our opinion it is in your interest to maintain a principle which is for the good of all — that anyone in danger should have just and equitable treatment and any advantage, even if not strictly his due, which he can secure by persuasion. This is your interest as much as ours, for your fall would involve you in a crushing punishment that would be a lesson to the world.

ATHENIANS: We have no apprehensions about the fate of our empire, if it did fall; those who rule other peoples, like the Lacedaemonians, are not formidable to a defeated enemy. Nor is it the Lacedaemonians with whom we are now contending: the danger is from subjects who of themselves may attack and conquer their rulers. But leave that danger to us to face. At the moment we shall prove that we have come in the interest of our empire and that in what we shall say we are seeking the safety of your state; for we wish you to become our subjects with least trouble to ourselves, and we would like you to survive in our interests as well as your own.

wants of Athenians

MELIANS: It may be your interest to be our masters; how can it be ours to be your slaves?

ATHENIANS: By submitting you would avoid a terrible fate, and we should gain by not destroying you.

MELIANS: Would you not agree to an arrangement under which we should keep out of the war, and be your friends instead of your enemies, but neutral?

Why can't they stay neutral

ATHENIANS: No; your hostility injures us less than your friendship. That, to our subjects, is an illustration of our weakness, while your hatred exhibits our power.

How ?

MELIANS: Is this the construction which your subjects put on it? Do they not distinguish between states in which you have no concern, and peoples who are most of them your colonies, and some conquered rebels?

ATHENIANS: They think that one nation has as good rights as another, but that some survive because they are strong and we are afraid to attack them. So, apart from the addition to our empire, your subjection would give us security: the fact that you are islanders (and weaker than others) makes it the more important that you should not get the better of the mistress of the sea.

reason

MELIANS: But do you see no safety in our neutrality? You debar us from the plea of justice and press us to submit to your interests, so we must expound our own, and try to convince you, if the two happen to coincide. Will you not make enemies of all neutral Powers when they see your conduct and reflect that some day you will attack them? Will not your action strengthen your existing opponents, and induce those who would otherwise never be your enemies to become so against their will?

ATHENIANS: No. The mainland states, secure in their freedom, will be slow to take defensive measures against us, and we do not consider them so formidable as independent island powers like yourselves, or subjects already smarting under our yoke. These are most likely to take a thoughtless step and bring themselves and us into obvious danger.

MELIANS: Surely then, if you are ready to risk so much to maintain your empire, and the enslaved peoples so much to escape from it, it would be criminal cowardice in us, who are still free, not to take any and every measure before submitting to slavery?

ATHENIANS: No, if you reflect calmly: for this is not a competition in heroism between equals, where your honor is at stake, but a question of self-preservation, to save you from a struggle with a far stronger Power.

MELIANS: Still, we know that in war fortune is more impartial than the disproportion in numbers might lead one to expect. If we submit at once, our position is desperate; if we fight, there is still a hope that we shall stand secure.

ATHENIANS: Hope encourages men to take risks; men in a strong position may follow her without ruin, if not without loss. But when they stake all that they have to the last coin (for she is a spendthrift), she reveals her real self in the hour of failure, and when her nature is known she leaves them without means of self-protection. You are weak, your future hangs on a turn of the scales; avoid the mistake most men make, who might save themselves by human means, and then, when visible hopes desert them, in their extremity turn to the invisible — prophecies and oracles and all those things which delude men with hopes, to their destruction.

MELIANS: We too, you can be sure, realize the difficulty of struggling against your power and against Fortune if she is not impartial. Still we trust that Heaven will not allow us to be worsted by Fortune, for in this quarrel we are right and you are wrong. Besides, we expect the support of Lacedaemon to supply the deficiencies in our strength, for she is bound to help us as her kinsmen, if for no other reason, and from a sense of honor. So our confidence is not entirely unreasonable.

ATHENIANS: As for divine favor, we think that we can count on it as much as you, for neither our claims nor our actions are inconsistent with what men believe about Heaven or desire for themselves. We believe that Heaven, and we know that men, by a natural law, always rule where they are stronger. We did not make that law nor were we the first to act on it; we found it existing, and it will exist forever, after we are gone; and we know that you and anyone else as strong as we are would do as we do. As to your expectations from Lacedaemon and your belief that she will help you from a sense of honor, we congratulate you on your innocence but we do not admire your folly. So far as they themselves and their national traditions are concerned, the Lacedaemonians are a highly virtuous people; as for their behavior to others, much might be said, but we can put it shortly by saying that, most obviously of all people we know, they identify their interests with justice and the pleasantest course with honor. Such principles do not favor your present irrational hopes of deliverance.

MELIANS: That is the chief reason why we have confidence in them now; in their own interest they will not wish to betray their own colonists and so help their enemies and destroy the confidence that their friends in Greece feel in them.

ATHENIANS: Apparently you do not realize that safety and self-interest go together, while the path of justice and honor is dangerous; and danger is a risk which the Lacedaemonians are little inclined to run.

MELIANS: Our view is that they would be more likely to run a risk in our case, and would regard it as less hazardous, because our nearness to Peloponnese makes it easier for them to act and our kinship gives them more confidence in us than in others.

ATHENIANS: Yes, but an intending ally looks not to the goodwill of those who invoke his aid but to marked superiority of real power, and of none is this truer than of the Lacedaemonians. They mistrust their own resources and attack their neighbors only when they have numerous allies, so it is not likely that, while we are masters of the sea, they would cross it to an island.

MELIANS: They might send others. The sea of Crete is large, and this will make it more difficult for its masters to capture hostile ships than for these to elude them safely. If they failed by sea, they would attack your country and those of your allies whom Brasidas* did not reach; and then you will have to fight not against a country in which you have no concern, but for your own country and your allies' lands.

ATHENIANS: Here experience may teach you like others, and you will learn that Athens has never abandoned a siege from fear of another foe. You said that you proposed to discuss the safety of your city, but we observe that in all your speeches you have never said a word on which any reasonable expectation of it could be founded. Your strength lies in deferred hopes; in comparison with

---

*Brasidas. A courageous and aggressive Spartan general who won many victories against the Athenians and their allies before he was killed in the tenth year of the war.

the forces now arrayed against you, your resources are too small for any hope of success. You will show a great want of judgment if you do not come to a more reasonable decision after we have withdrawn. Surely you will not fall back on the idea of honor, which has been the ruin of so many when danger and disgrace were staring them in the face. How often, when men have seen the fate to which they were tending, have they been enslaved by a phrase and drawn by the power of this seductive word to fall of their own free will into irreparable disaster, bringing on themselves by their folly a greater dishonor than fortune could inflict! If you are wise, you will avoid that fate. The greatest of cities makes you a fair offer, to keep your own land and become her tributary ally: there is no dishonor in that. The choice between war and safety is given you; do not obstinately take the worse alternative. The most successful people are those who stand up to their equals, behave properly to their superiors, and treat their inferiors fairly. Think it over when we withdraw, and reflect once and again that you have only one country, and that its prosperity or ruin depends on one decision.

[margin, handwritten: What is fair?]

THE ATHENIANS now withdrew from the conference; and the Melians, left to themselves, came to a decision corresponding with what they had maintained in the discussion, and answered, "Our resolution, Athenians, is unaltered. We will not in a moment deprive of freedom a city that has existed for seven hundred years; we put our trust in the fortune by which the gods have preserved it until now, and in the help of men, that is, of the Lacedaemonians; and so we will try and save ourselves. Meanwhile we invite you to allow us to be friends to you and foes to neither party, and to retire from our country after making such a treaty as shall seem fit to us both."

[margin, handwritten: still looking to be neutral]

Such was the answer of the Melians. The Athenians broke up the conference saying, "To judge from your decision, you are unique in regarding the future as more certain than the present and in allowing your wishes to convert the unseen into reality; and as you have staked most on, and trusted most in, the Lacedaemonians, your fortune, and your hopes, so will you be most completely deceived."

The Athenian envoys now returned to the army; and as the Melians showed no signs of yielding, the generals at once began hostilities, and drew a line of circumvallation round the Melians, dividing the work among the different states. Subsequently the Athenians returned with most of their army, leaving behind them a certain number of their own citizens and of the allies to keep guard by land and sea. The force thus left stayed on and besieged the place.

Meanwhile the Athenians at Pylos took so much plunder from the Lacedaemonians that the latter, although they still refrained from breaking off the treaty and going to war with Athens, proclaimed that any of their people that chose might plunder the Athenians. The Corinthians also commenced hostilities with the Athenians for private quarrels of their own; but the rest of the Peloponnesians stayed quiet. Meanwhile the Melians in a night attack took the part of the Athenian lines opposite the market, killed some of its garrison, and brought in corn and as many useful stores as they could. Then, retiring, they remained inactive, while the Athenians took measures to keep better guard in future. Summer was now over. The next winter the Lacedaemonians intended to invade the Argive territory, but on arriving at the frontier found the sacrifices for crossing unfavorable, and went back again. This intention of theirs made the Argives suspicious of certain of their fellow citizens, some of whom they arrested; others, however, escaped them. About the same time the Melians again took another part of the Athenian lines which were but feebly garrisoned. In consequence reinforcements were sent from Athens, and the siege was now pressed

vigorously; there was some treachery in the town, and the
Melians surrendered at discretion to the Athenians, who
put to death all the grown men whom they took, and sold
the women and children for slaves; subsequently they sent
out five hundred settlers and colonized the island. ❖

would the fate of the Melians have
been any different if they had submitted initially?

E whose interpretation of reality valid— M or A?

- Is honor the ruin of the Melians?
- Is the Athenians interpretation of natural
  law correct?

- Why did the Athenians feel the Melians had wronged them

- p. 83-84 Why hostility injures them less than friendship?

- why does hope encourage risk (Athenians)

- Do the Melians indeed have a choice in the
  disposition of their country?

- Why were the islanders considered weaker than others?
      E - are they?

- What part does hope play in the ruin of the Melians?

Distinguishing Factual, Interpretive, and Evaluative Questions

JACK AND THE BEANSTALK

DIRECTIONS: For each of the following questions, indicate with an "F," "I," or "E" whether the question is factual, interpretive, or evaluative.

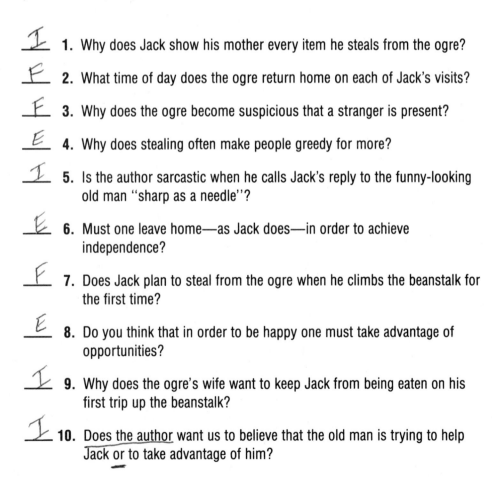

I   **1.** Why does Jack show his mother every item he steals from the ogre?

F   **2.** What time of day does the ogre return home on each of Jack's visits?

F   **3.** Why does the ogre become suspicious that a stranger is present?

E   **4.** Why does stealing often make people greedy for more?

I   **5.** Is the author sarcastic when he calls Jack's reply to the funny-looking old man "sharp as a needle"?

E   **6.** Must one leave home—as Jack does—in order to achieve independence?

F   **7.** Does Jack plan to steal from the ogre when he climbs the beanstalk for the first time?

E   **8.** Do you think that in order to be happy one must take advantage of opportunities?

I   **9.** Why does the ogre's wife want to keep Jack from being eaten on his first trip up the beanstalk?

I   **10.** Does the <u>author</u> want us to believe that the old man is trying to help Jack or to take advantage of him?

II

Asking Follow-up Questions

A GAME OF CATCH

DIRECTIONS: Each sequence below consists of a question and a response. For each sequence, write the follow-up question you would ask. Your question should pursue <u>both</u> the participant's response and the leader's question.

1. **Leader:** Does the author want us to believe that Glennie and Monk treat Scho unfairly?

   Participant: No, on the whole they behave very well toward a pushy kid.

   Your Follow-up Question:

   Why do you believe that Scho is a pushy kid? What did they do to Scho that is fair play?

2. **Leader:** Why do Monk and Glennie ignore what Scho says after he finds a seat in the tree?

   Participant: What did he say? *Can anyone tell us what he said?*

   Your Follow-up Question:

   Look back at page 77, How did M & G react towards Scho when he went into the tree?

   (or rephrase)

3. **Leader:** Why does Monk begin to throw the ball to Glennie once or twice before he gives Scho his grounder?

   Participant: Because Scho failed to catch one of the balls that Monk threw him.

   Your Follow-up Question:

   → Where in the story did Scho miss the ball?
   Does Scho miss the ball before or after Mon
     kept throwing the ball to Glennie?
   (follow up w/ positive when he catches his mistak

   or turn to group depending on group
     sometimes group can be too harsh

4. **Leader:** Just before Scho falls, why does the author describe his voice as "exuberant and panicky"?

   Participant: I don't think I could have those two feelings at the same time.

   Your Follow-up Question:

   Let's look at one at a time, What
   would make Scho exuberant?
   Why would Scho feel panicky then
     (what events)

   or How do you think Scho is feeling?

[handwritten marginal notes:] child aside to read story if they've never read it.

phrase question

ect to text

a reread

der may not have

ed story, and doesn't

t to participate

k why, listen to

y their isn't an answer or

courage finding out

y they didn't like

tory — responsible for

n opinions — defend

5. Leader: Why does Scho enlarge the scope of his game at the end of the story?

Participant: I don't know.

Your Follow-up Question:

[handwritten:] what is Scho's game?
what does Scho want to accomplish?
Refer to last line of story — what does Scho mean?

6. Leader: Why does Scho tease the boys mainly while he is in the tree?

Participant 1: Playing his game from the tree gives Scho a false sense of power because he is looking down on Glennie and Monk.

Participant 2: Scho feels safe from any attempt of Glennie and Monk's to shut him up.

Your Follow-up Question: *[handwritten:]* direct ~~to~~ each participate

[handwritten:]
1 - why is it a false sense of power?

2 - ~~Wes~~ What makes you think that
Scho feels safe?
Do you think your ~~idea~~ answer is similar
to #1?

The Junior Great Books Reading and Discussion Series

The second-semester series are intended for Junior Great Books groups that require additional reading selections during the second part of the school year. They are not recommended for use with newly formed groups.

*Selection
†Based on traditional material

SERIES 2

Two Fables
La Fontaine, Aesop

The Happy Lion
Louise Fatio

Cinderella
Charles Perrault

The Monkey and the Crocodile
Ellen C. Babbitt

The Mouse Bride
Lucia Turnbull†

Stone Soup
Marcia Brown†

The Terrible Leak
Yoshiko Uchida†

How the Camel Got His Hump
Rudyard Kipling

Jack and the Beanstalk
Joseph Jacobs†

The Man with the Wen
Idries Shah†

Tom-Tit-Tot
Flora Annie Steel†

The Velveteen Rabbit
Margery Williams

SERIES 3

First Semester

The Master Cat
(or: Puss-in-Boots)
Charles Perrault

The Fisherman and His Wife
Jacob and Wilhelm Grimm†

The Ugly Duckling
Hans Christian Andersen

Caporushes
Flora Annie Steel†

The Monster Who Grew Small
Joan Grant

The Brave Little Tailor
Jacob and Wilhelm Grimm†

Ooka and the Honest Thief
I. G. Edmonds

The Green Man
Gail E. Haley

The Fire on the Mountain
Harold Courlander and Wolf Leslau†

Beauty and the Beast
Madame de Villeneuve

Ellen's Lion
Crockett Johnson

The Mousewife
Rumer Godden

Second Semester

The Black Heart of Indri
Dorothy Hoge

It's All the Fault of Adam
Barbara Walker†

Jean Labadie's Big Black Dog
Natalie Savage Carlson

The Little Humpbacked Horse
Post Wheeler†

The Jackal and the Partridge
Flora Annie Steel†

The Snowman
Hans Christian Andersen

The Tale of the Three Storytellers
James Krüss

Woman's Wit
Howard Pyle

The Stone Crusher of Banjang
Harold Courlander†

How the Tortoise Became
Ted Hughes

The Invisible Child
Tove Jansson

The Wind in the Willows*
Kenneth Grahame

SERIES 4

First Semester

The Red Balloon
Albert Lamorisse

The Emperor's New Clothes
Hans Christian Andersen

The Devoted Friend
Oscar Wilde

Allah Will Provide
Robert Gilstrap and Irene Estabrook†

Vasilissa the Beautiful
Post Wheeler†

Prince Rabbit
A. A. Milne

The Story of Dr. Dolittle*
Hugh Lofting

The Imp in the Basket
Natalie Babbitt

Mr. Toad*
Kenneth Grahame

The Goldfish
Eleanor Farjeon

The Elephant's Child
Rudyard Kipling

Ali Baba and the Forty Thieves
Charlotte Dixon†

Second Semester

How the Donkey and the Elephant Became
Ted Hughes

The Wicked Tricks of Tyl Uilenspiegel*
Jay Williams

Mr. Singer's Nicknames
James Krüss

The Story of Wang Li
Elizabeth Coatsworth

Thunder, Elephant, and Dorobo
Humphrey Harman†

A Likely Place
Paula Fox

The Enchanted Sticks
Steven J. Meyers

Wisdom's Wages and Folly's Pay
Howard Pyle

The Battle of the Frogs and the Mice
George Martin

The Hemulen Who Loved Silence
Tove Jansson

What the Neighbors Did
Philippa Pearce

Alice's Adventures in Wonderland*
Lewis Carroll

SERIES 5

First Semester

Charles
Shirley Jackson

The Nightingale
Hans Christian Andersen

Thank You, M'am
Langston Hughes

Fables
Leo Tolstoy

The Happy Prince
Oscar Wilde

Fresh
Philippa Pearce

Echo and Narcissus
Kathleen Lines†

All Summer in a Day
Ray Bradbury

Kaddo's Wall
Harold Courlander and George Herzog†

The Fifty-First Dragon
Heywood Broun

Spit Nolan
Bill Naughton

Maurice's Room
Paula Fox

Second Semester

The Ghost Cat
Donna Hill

The Prince and the Goose Girl
Elinor Mordaunt

Podhu and Aruwa
Humphrey Harman†

Lucky Boy
Philippa Pearce

Dita's Story
Mary Q. Steele

Alberic the Wise
Norton Juster

The Secret of the Hattifatteners
Tove Jansson

The White Falcon
Charlton Ogburn

The Mysteries of the Cabala
Isaac Bashevis Singer

The Magic Jacket
Walter de la Mare

Lenny's Red-Letter Day
Bernard Ashley

The Bat-Poet
Randall Jarrell

SERIES 6

Through the Tunnel
Doris Lessing

The Parsley Garden
William Saroyan

The Gun Without a Bang
Robert Sheckley

The Alligators
John Updike

I Don't See George Anymore
Philip Oakes

The Jungle Books*
Rudyard Kipling

The Zodiacs
Jay Neugeboren

Day of the Butterfly
Alice Munro

The Veldt
Ray Bradbury

A Game of Catch
Richard Wilbur

To Build a Fire
Jack London

As the Night the Day
Abioseh Nicol

Second Semester

Raymond's Run
Toni Cade Bambara

The Secret of the Yellow House
Anatoly Aleksin

I Just Kept On Smiling
Simon Burt

Through the Looking-Glass*
Lewis Carroll

Star Food
Ethan Canin

The Sand Castle
Mary Lavin

The Last Great Snake
Mary Q. Steele

The Secret Lion
Alberto Alvaro Rios

The Jungle Books: Letting in the Jungle
Rudyard Kipling

The Jungle Books: The Spring Running
Rudyard Kipling

Soumchi
Amos Oz

(continued on next page)

The Junior Great Books Reading and Discussion Series

SERIES 7

Harrison Bergeron
Kurt Vonnegut, Jr.

The Idealist
Frank O'Connor

The Stone Boy
Gina Berriault

Sir Tristram and the Fair
Iseult
Roger Lancelyn Green†

The White Circle
John Bell Clayton

Bad Characters
Jean Stafford

The Cat and the Coffee
Drinkers
Max Steele

The Camel, the Lion,
the Leopard, the
Crow, and the Jackal
Ramsay Wood†

Gaston
William Saroyan

The Rocking-Horse
Winner
D.H. Lawrence

Spomono
Alan Paton

The Adventures of
Huckleberry Finn*
Mark Twain

SERIES 8

The Ledge
Lawrence Sargent Hall

Sucker
Carson McCullers

The Summer of the
Beautiful White
Horse
William Saroyan

Rufus
James Agee

Boys and Girls
Alice Munro

A Stick of Green Candy
Jane Bowles

Mateo Falcone
Prosper Mérimée

The Griffin and the
Minor Canon
Frank R. Stockton

The Destructors
Graham Greene

Baby Deer
Sunil Gangopadhyaya

Debbie Go Home
Alan Paton

Dr. Jekyll and Mr. Hyde
Robert Louis Stevenson

SERIES 9

The Lottery
Shirley Jackson

A Mystery of Heroism
Stephen Crane

A Bird in the House
Margaret Laurence

Miriam
Truman Capote

The Guest
Albert Camus

The Time Machine
H.G. Wells

End of the Game
Julio Cortázar

Mumu
Ivan Turgenev

The Outlaws
Selma Lagerlöf

The End of the Party
Graham Greene

The Evildoer
Anton Chekhov

The Loneliness of the
Long-Distance
Runner
Alan Sillitoe

SERIES 10

Why War?*
Sigmund Freud

The Melian Dialogue*
Thucydides

The Social Me*
William James

Rothschild's Fiddle
Anton Chekhov

Concerning the Division
of Labor*
Adam Smith

Chelkash
Maxim Gorky

How an Aristocracy
May Be Created by
Industry*
Alexis de Tocqueville

Observation and
Experiment*
Claude Bernard

Everything That Rises
Must Converge
Flannery O'Connor

An Essay in Aesthetics*
Roger Fry

An Outpost of Progress
Joseph Conrad

On Studying*
José Ortega y Gasset

SERIES 11

Politics*
Aristotle

Of Commonwealth*
Thomas Hobbes

Barn Burning
William Faulkner

Of Civil Government*
John Locke

In Exile
Anton Chekhov

The Declaration of
Independence

Equality*
Isaiah Berlin

Sorrow-Acre
Isak Dinesen

Why Americans Are
Often So Restless*
Alexis de Tocqueville

After the Ball
Leo Tolstoy

Habit*
William James

The Overcoat
Nikolai Gogol

SERIES 12

On Happiness*
Aristotle

Habits and Will*
John Dewey

Happiness
Mary Lavin

Crito*
Plato

On Liberty*
John Stuart Mill

Conscience
Immanuel Kant

A Hunger Artist
Franz Kafka

Of the Limits of
Government*
John Locke

Antigone
Sophocles

Why Great Revolutions
Will Become Rare*
Alexis de Tocqueville

A Room of One's Own*
Virginia Woolf

In Dreams Begin
Responsibilities
Delmore Schwartz

The Adult Great Books Reading and Discussion Series

*Indicates complete work. All other selections are portions of larger works.

FIRST SERIES

Chekhov
*Rothschild's Fiddle**

Aristotle
On Happiness

Plato
*The Apology**

Conrad
*Heart of Darkness**

Kant
Conscience

Marx
Alienated Labour

Bible
Genesis

Freud
Civilization and Its Discontents

Rousseau
The Social Contract

Darwin
The Moral Sense of Man and the Lower Animals

Shakespeare
*Othello**

Hume
Of Justice and Injustice

Tocqueville
The Power of the Majority

Simmel
Individual Freedom

Sophocles
*Antigone**

SECOND SERIES

Plato
*The Crito**

Dewey
The Virtues

Euripides
*Iphigeneia at Aulis**

Aristotle
Politics

Dostoevsky
*Notes from the Underground**

Bible
Exodus

Hobbes
Origin of Government

Melville
*Billy Budd, Sailor**

Smith
Wealth of Nations

Shakespeare
*Antony and Cleopatra**

Kierkegaard
The Knight of Faith

Herodotus
The Persian Wars

Locke
Of Civil Government

Swift
Gulliver's Travels

Thoreau
*Civil Disobedience**

THIRD SERIES

Dewey
Habits and Will

Mill
On Liberty

Shakespeare
*Hamlet**

Bible
The Gospel of Mark

Thucydides
History of the Peloponnesian War

Clausewitz
What Is War?

Chekhov
*Uncle Vanya**

Maimonides
On Evil

Homer
The Iliad

Montesquieu
Principles of Government

Chaucer
The Canterbury Tales

Aeschylus:
*Agamemnon**

James
*The Beast in the Jungle**

Machiavelli
The Prince

Tolstoy
*The Death of Ivan Ilych**

FOURTH SERIES

Schopenhauer
The Indestructibility of Our Inner Nature

Euripides
*Medea**

Weber
The Spirit of Capitalism

Molière
*The Misanthrope**

Gibbon
The Decline and Fall of the Roman Empire

Bible
Job

Mill
Utilitarianism

Shaw
*Caesar and Cleopatra**

St. Augustine
The City of God

Plato
Symposium

Montaigne
*Of Experience**

Diderot
Rameau's Nephew

Shakespeare
*The Tempest**

Hamilton, Jay, Madison
The Federalist

Gogol
*The Overcoat**

FIFTH SERIES

Bible
Ecclesiastes

Sophocles
*Oedipus the King**

Freud
On Dreams

Kafka
*The Metamorphosis**

Goethe
*Faust, Part One**

Kant
First Principles of Morals

Flaubert
*A Simple Heart**

Hume
Of Personal Identity

Nietzsche
Thus Spoke Zarathustra

Dante
The Inferno

Burke
Reflections on the Revolution in France

Adams
The Education of Henry Adams

Shakespeare
*King Lear**

Aristotle
On Tragedy

Plato
The Republic